The
SIMPLE
MESSAGE
of the
CROSS

MARC BAKER

TWO BLESSED BEARS PUBLISHING
Bradenton, FL

The Simple Message of the Cross
ISBN: 979-8-9887462-4-9 (paperback)
ISBN: 979-8-9887462-5-6 (eBook)
Copyright © 2024 by Marc Baker
Bradenton, FL 34203

Published by:
Two Blessed Bears Publishing
Bradenton, FL 34203
www.mbmediaministries.net

I am crucified with Christ: nevertheless I live; yet not I, but Christ liveth in me: and the life which I now live in the flesh I live by the faith of the Son of God, who loved me, and gave himself for me.

GALATIANS 2:20 (KJV, EMPHASIS ADDED)

Contents

Introduction

Then Jesus said to His disciples, "If anyone desires to come after Me, let him deny himself, and take up his cross, and follow Me."

MATTHEW 16:24

The cross of Christ has been depicted in art, as jewelry, and in many other ways. Do you understand its message? In my experience, the majority do not. Unfortunately, the cross has largely become a religious cliché in our culture. It is rare to hear any more than a brief mention of it in our day of faith, healing, and prosperity messages. I do believe God desires for us to prosper and be in health, but I am concerned that our message has changed from the one delivered by the early church. It seems to have moved away from the gospel of Jesus Christ and instead become focused on avoiding confrontation and creating a climate of comfort for those attending our services.

Sinners and Christians alike have some form of awareness of the cross. We know Jesus died a horrible death on it. We also know that His death enabled us to receive forgiveness for our sins. But is that all there is to the message of the cross? The Holy Spirit has helped me see that it is not. The message extends beyond our Lord's death to the life we are called to live as followers of Christ. The cross was the place where the judgment of God was poured out on Him. It was also a beautiful expression of God's love, mercy, and goodness toward humanity.

Our focus in this book will be primarily on Paul's references to the cross. He provides us a different picture than what we find in the Gospels and book of Acts. Those books primarily focus on the actual cross and crucifixion. Matthew, Mark, Luke, and John mention the cross in various ways without providing much more detail. They reference the crucifixion and provide details of Jesus' being nailed to it and how He was treated as He hung on it. Paul approaches the subject from a different viewpoint that we are going to examine in detail in the pages ahead.

Chapter 1

The Cross and the Covenants

But now He has obtained a more excellent ministry,
inasmuch as He is also Mediator of a better covenant,
which was established on better promises.

HEBREWS 8:6

During my early years as a Christian, I faced many challenges because I was part of a church that did not have a proper understanding of the cross. Their teachings mixed aspects of the old and new covenants, which created a confusing perception of God in my mind. An unhealthy fear of God plagued me, as I believed that even the slightest mistake could lead to God's judgment falling on me. The concept of God's mercy was never emphasized, and my relationship with Him became based on works and deeds focused on gaining His love. Without realizing it, I had adopted an approach to God that Jesus died to set me free from.

I have noticed that many people in the church today are confused about the difference between the old and new covenants just like I was. Some have been exposed to ministers that mix the two just like those I sat under while growing up. There is more that differentiates the two than just a blank page between the Old and New Testaments of our Bibles. The tendency to combine the two covenants often leads to the belief that God is constantly angry with us and has high expectations that are almost impossible to meet. This has created a mental barrier for many Christians, making it difficult for them to establish a relationship with God. In reality, the cross provides freedom from this Old Testament mentality to those who gain revelation of the cross's message.

It is true that the Old Testament contains accounts of God's wrath being poured out in judgment on humanity. Examples of this can be found in God's judging Egypt (Exodus 7–11), Israel in the desert (Ezekiel 20:13), and Sodom and Gomorrah (Genesis 18-19). However, we must remember that these events occurred before the cross. At that time, Jesus had not yet been crucified, and God's dealings with humanity were different than they are today. The wrath of God was poured out on Jesus at the cross, and this has resulted in a significant change in our relationship with Him. Unfortunately, many Christians fail to grasp this truth.

The Cross Is Our Open Door

I fear we are not correctly teaching the message of the cross. As a result, many Christians struggle with the same issues I faced in how they approach God. Our focus is on old covenant mentalities, which are not necessarily wrong if taught in the proper context. However, the old covenant occurred before the cross and is therefore incomplete. Hebrews 8:6 tells us the new covenant is "a better covenant, which was established on better promises." I am not advocating throwing out the Old Testament; rather, I am saying we need to become more established in our revelation of the new covenant.

The cross opened the door for us to develop a relationship with God that was impossible for Old Testament saints to experience. Understanding this is important, as our view of the Old Testament can be distorted otherwise. My approach to God while growing up is a prime example. No one told me that God chose me in Christ "before the foundation of the world" (Ephesians 1:4), predestined me to be adopted into His family as a son (Ephesians 1:5), or that Jesus' sacrifice on the cross made me "accepted in the Beloved" (Ephesians 1:6). My lack of knowledge of these New Testament truths caused me to view God as being angry at me because I was viewing Him through an old covenant lens.

He Will Never Leave Us

As a Christian, when you confessed Jesus as your Lord, you were sealed into Him by the Holy Spirit (Ephesians 1:13). This seal is unbreakable and cannot be removed by Satan, because he would have to overcome the Spirit to do so. God has promised to always be with us and never abandon us (Hebrews 13:5). The seal in Christ is a way for God to ensure that this promise is always kept. Every Christian has been immersed into Jesus (1 Corinthians 12:13) and then sealed into Him. Spiritually, we are immersed in His presence and cannot escape it.

The New Testament is filled with promises that assure us of the perpetual presence of Father, Jesus, and the Holy Spirit in our lives. One example is Hebrews 13:5, which reminds us that God has said, "I will never leave you nor forsake you." Another example can be found in John 14:16, where Jesus said of the Holy Spirit that He would "abide with [us] forever." These promises were not available to those who lived under the old covenant. They could lose God's presence, but we cannot. Our relationship with God has been transformed by the blood of Jesus, which was shed at the cross. Because of His blood, we are assured of God's constant presence in our lives.

It is true that sin creates a barrier between us and God. However, Jesus removed that barrier by sacrificing Himself on the cross, thereby opening the door for us to live in the presence of God. It is important to note that removing the barrier does not mean we should allow sin to remain in our lives. Although sin cannot change God's opinion of us, it can affect our fellowship with Him by causing our hearts to become calloused to His presence. Fortunately, the Holy Spirit was sent to help us. I have found that the more time I spend in fellowship with Him, the less of an issue sin becomes in my life. There is something about quietly sitting with the Spirit and the Word of God that motivates us to live a holy life.

We don't have to wait until we reach heaven to have a relationship with our heavenly Father. He invites us to approach His throne confidently, expecting mercy and grace (Hebrews 4:16). Many Christians believe that they must perform religious rituals to earn God's favor, but this is not true. According to Revelation 4:11, we were created to please Him. The cross made it possible for us to approach the throne and have fellowship with God. Our ability to approach Him is based solely on Christ's performance at the cross. Our sins, mistakes, and failures won't change His opinion of us because it is based on Christ's redemptive work alone.

The Anointing Follows the Presence

In Acts 10:38, Luke states that "God anointed Jesus of Nazareth with the Holy Spirit and the power." Here's a question for you: If you are sealed in Christ by the same Holy Spirit that God anointed Jesus with, wouldn't it make sense that you have access to the same anointing that Jesus had? This is something that a lot of Christians have never considered. That's why many people spend hours praying to God, asking Him to anoint them, unaware that He already did the moment they were born again.

Our religious traditions often shift our focus from Jesus and place it on our own performance. As a result, we tend to believe that we must do something to earn the favor that Jesus has already given us. This belief can manifest in different ways, especially in our prayer lives. Many Christians believe that they need to work to earn God's anointing, and this can cause them to spend countless hours praying, hoping to receive the anointing as a reward. However, this mindset misses the point that God has already anointed us. All we need to do is commit time to fellowship with the Holy Spirit and the Word to tap into the anointing that we already have.

Let's examine an example from Luke 4:18–19 to help illustrate.

> The Spirit of the LORD *is* upon Me, because He has anointed Me to preach the gospel to *the* poor; He has sent Me to heal the brokenhearted, to proclaim liberty to *the* captives and recovery of sight to *the* blind, *to* set at liberty those who are oppressed; to proclaim the acceptable year of the LORD.

In the temple, Jesus announced to the people that the Spirit of God had anointed Him. Interestingly, there was no mention of His praying to open the meeting. This is because Jesus knew He was already anointed even before walking into the meeting. As recorded in Luke 4:16, Jesus had a custom of reading from the book of Isaiah in the synagogue. He believed that the prophecy from Isaiah 61:1–3 would be fully manifested in the meeting. This shows the confidence Jesus had in His anointing. As believers who are also anointed by the same Spirit, do we have the same level of confidence of having the same anointing?

Chapter 2

The Self-Righteous Mindset

For Christ did not send me to baptize, but to preach the gospel, not with wisdom of words, lest the cross of Christ should be made of no effect. For the message of the cross is foolishness to those who are perishing, but to us who are being saved it is the power of God.

1 CORINTHIANS 1:17–18

In the previous chapter, I asked you a question: How confident are you that God has anointed you with the same anointing that Jesus had? This is an important question that you should take time to consider. Many people have not given this much thought, which is why there are so many prayer meetings where believers gather to ask God for His anointing. In the previous chapter, we looked at Luke 4:18–19 and saw that it was Jesus' custom to read from Isaiah 61:1–3. There is no evidence that Jesus ever questioned the anointing on His life. He was certain that He was anointed and declared it without hesitation. It is only when we reach the same level of certainty that we will see the same miraculous demonstrations that He saw in His ministry.

I have attended many prayer meetings where the focus was on the power of God. I've also heard many messages about it over the years. One day I was at home crying out to God for a touch of His power, and the Holy Spirit stopped me. He asked me to read Romans

1:16. Although I had heard this passage quoted before, I had never really spent much time meditating on it. In this verse, Paul tells us that the gospel "is the power of God to salvation for everyone who believes." This statement is also echoed in 1 Corinthians 1:18 (KJV), where Paul tells us that "the preaching of the cross is to them that perish foolishness; but unto us which are saved it is the power of God." In other words, the power of God is available to anyone who meditates on His Word and until it becomes revelation knowledge. We do not need to pray, fast, or jump through any other religious hoops to access it.

How We Empty the Power from the Message of the Cross

According to Paul, we are the ones who render the gospel message to be of "none effect" in our lives (1 Corinthians 1:17, KJV). This is a sobering statement. Paul was describing a state in which the message of the cross is emptied of power. The Word of God contains the power of God. We can only access that power, though, by dedicating time to meditating on God's Word and by spending time in fellowship with the Spirit of God. This is an essential point that we must not forget. Paul explains in 1 Corinthians 1:17 that when we rely on our own wisdom and natural understanding to deliver the gospel message, we cause it to lose its power.

God sent Paul to "preach the gospel" (1 Corinthians 1:17) just as He sends us today. This means that we are tasked with sharing the complete message of the good news of Jesus' sacrifice for our sins. The gospel of Christ is the power of God to save us, as stated in Romans 1:16. *Soteria* is the Greek word for *salvation* that is used in the verse, which encompasses much more than just being saved from sin. It also encompasses our welfare, prosperity, deliverance, preservation, and safety, which are all found in Christ alone.

Many religious leaders and organizations nowadays think that we don't require the miraculous power of God anymore. This idea is being taught in seminaries, causing many people who were once passionate about God to graduate without experiencing His power or anointing. This reminds me of Paul's statement in 1 Corinthians 1:17 (KJV):

> For Christ sent me not to baptize, but to preach the gospel: not with wisdom of words, lest the cross of Christ should be made of none effect.

People who pursue ministry often receive extensive training in theology and doctrine. While education is important, individuals seem to be spending too much time acquiring knowledge about God in seminary or Bible college, leaving little time to cultivate their relationship with Him. As a result, their connection with God can be superficial.

A minister who only possesses knowledge in their head will lead their congregation toward religious traditions. This makes the cross of Christ "of none effect," as Paul describes. The Greek word translated as "none effect" indicates that the power of the cross has been drained away. Our intellectualism has deprived many Christians of experiencing a close relationship with God and His divine power.

The term *preach* in 1 Corinthians 1:17 refers to an expression of God's thoughts through a human vessel yielded to the anointing of the Holy Spirit. Paul further explains this concept in Galatians 1:6–9 (KJV):

> I marvel that ye are so soon removed from him that called you into the grace of Christ unto another gospel: which is not another; but there be some that trouble you, and would pervert the gospel of Christ. But though we, or an angel from heaven, preach any other gospel unto you than that which we have preached unto you, let him be accursed. As we said before, so say I now again, if any

man preach any other gospel unto you than that ye have
received, let him be accursed.

It is essential for anyone who is called to teach God's Word to
always keep these verses in mind. Many people have been turned
away from the message of the cross by well-intentioned ministers
who teach knowledge they learned from academic studies but have
never been exposed to the concept of receiving revelation knowledge
directly from the Holy Spirit. This knowledge can only be received
through meditation on the Word and fellowship with the Spirit. It
is worth noting that Paul twice tells his readers in these verses that
anyone guilty of doing this should be accursed. This is a serious
thought to consider.

Full Payment for
Sin Has Been Made

We often discuss that Jesus carried the weight of our sins at the cross.
While this is true, it seems that many Christians do not understand
He paid the total price for their sins. As a result, many of us try to
earn God's favor and miss the fact that it has already been given to
us through the death, burial, and resurrection of Jesus. According to
Paul, we were chosen in Christ "before the foundation of the world,
that we should be holy and without blame" before God, who "predestined us to adoption as sons by Jesus Christ to Himself" (Ephesians 1:4–5). Our position and selection by God are made possible
by the price Jesus paid on the cross to free us from the chains of condemnation and sin. The details of this payment will be further discussed in chapters 13 and 14.

Under the Law, a person's standing before God was based on their
goodness and the good works they did in His service. There was a
problem though. If they failed in even the smallest area, the Law

considered them guilty of breaking every part of it (James 2:10). The cross changed the equation. It opened the door for us to be accepted into God's presence without consideration of our goodness or good works. Our acceptance by Him today is based solely on the merit of Jesus' redemptive work accomplished on the cross. Unfortunately, there are many Christians today who seem to believe (on at least a subconscious level) that the payment made was not complete. It is almost as if they think He made a down payment, and they are now required by God to pay the remaining debt due for their sin.

Jesus told His disciples that our traditions would render the Word of God powerless in our lives (Mark 7:13). There are whole denominations today that teach an incomplete redemption. This is the source of false beliefs that lead people to assume God expects something from them before He will be willing to accept them. I have heard ministers list things such as strict adherence to spiritual disciplines, faithful church attendance, or participation in the sacrament of communion as requirements to meet His expectations. I am not minimizing these things, but they are not required to earn God's acceptance, as He has already accepted us in Christ Jesus regardless of the things we do, or do not do, for Him (Ephesians 1:6).

The Benefits Provided in the Cross

It astounds me to recall how so few people I've met over the years have a revelation of the benefits made available to them through the cross. Paul tells us God has already "blessed us with every spiritual blessing in the heavenly places in Christ" (Ephesians 1:3). He then provides us a list of examples:

- We have been chosen by God in Christ from "before the foundation of the world, that we should be holy and without blame before Him in love" (Ephesians 1:4).

- God "predestined us to adoption as sons by Jesus Christ to Himself, according to the good pleasure of His will" (Ephesians 1:5).

- We were made to be accepted by God in Christ Jesus (Ephesians 1:6).

- God redeemed us through the blood of Jesus and forgave our sins "according to the riches of His grace" (Ephesians 1:7).

- God has made Jesus to "abound toward us in all wisdom and prudence" (Ephesians 1:8).

- The mystery of God's will is revealed to us in Christ "according to His good pleasure which He purposed in Himself" (Ephesians 1:9).

- In the dispensation of times, God will gather us to Himself in Christ (Ephesians 1:10).

- We were predestined to receive an inheritance "according to the purpose of Him who works all things according to the counsel of His will" (Ephesians 1:11).

These are some of the benefits that are available to anyone who trusts in Christ as their Lord and Savior. In Ephesians 1:13, Paul explains that anyone who hears the gospel message and believes in it is sealed with the Holy Spirit of promise in Jesus. Through the Spirit, every Christian is baptized into Christ (Galatians 3:27) and is freed from condemnation because of their position in Jesus. However, this is only possible if they yield to the Holy Spirit and do not allow themselves to walk according to the flesh (Romans 8:1).

Freedom Is Found in Christ Alone

Paul warns us in Galatians 5:1–6 of the dangers faced by those who try to add their efforts to the message of the cross:

> Stand fast therefore in the liberty by which Christ has made us free, and do not be entangled again with a yoke of bondage. Indeed I, Paul, say to you that if you become circumcised, Christ will profit you nothing. And I testify again to every man who becomes circumcised that he is a debtor to keep the whole law. You have become estranged from Christ, you who *attempt to* be justified by law; you have fallen from grace. For we through the Spirit eagerly wait for the hope of righteousness by faith. For in Christ Jesus neither circumcision nor uncircumcision avails anything, but faith working through love.

I am always amazed by these verses where Paul speaks of being circumcised. In a figurative sense, he describes a condition of being cut off from Christ. This is why he warns us that those who entangle themselves with religious traditions will find no profit in their Christian walk. In this context, "profit" describes a condition that provides no help or value. Paul uses the word *circumcise* to warn us that those who turn to self-righteous works will find themselves in a position where they are cut off from Christ. According to John 1:4 and John 4:14, life flows from Jesus, and it is safe to say that those who have been cut off from Him are also cut off from experiencing His life. Our failure to abide in Christ will result in a fruitless life (John 15:6).

Some ministers believe that by not living a holy life or by failing to follow God's rules, we are diminishing the power of the cross. However, Galatians 5:1–6 shows us that this statement is incorrect. Pursuing religious works like those taught by these ministers renders the cross powerless. Through His death, burial, and resurrection, Jesus has already made us acceptable in God's eyes (Ephesians 1:3–6). We cannot change this fact. As I mentioned, setting religious requirements for holy living removes us from the life that flows from Jesus. Those who accept His grace and strive to have a relationship with Him will find themselves living holy lives as an act of love for the one who redeemed them rather than a mere fulfillment of religious obligation.

The Sin of Self-Righteousness

What is the worst sin a person can commit? The answer varies depending on who you ask. Everyone has their own perception of sin, which affects how they answer the question. Some might say adultery is the worst sin, while others might say it is drunkenness. Christians, in particular, can be very defensive about their views on sin. I even found myself trapped in this mindset due to the religious teachings I received early in my Christian journey.

In the past, I used to believe that murder was the worst sin a person could commit. However, my opinion changed over time, and I began to consider other sins equally bad, if not worse. As a result, my faith in God and my belief structure became unstable. One day, while praying, the Holy Spirit interrupted me and asked why I believed that God would consider one sin worse than any other. This made me reconsider my perspective and helped me understand that all sins are equal in the eyes of God.

From God's perspective, sin causes our hearts to harden. This holds true whether the sin is a small white lie or a serious crime like murder. Every sin gradually builds a barrier in our hearts that prevents us from drawing closer to God and causes our hearts to become hardened to Him. In my opinion, the sin of self-righteousness has the most damaging effect on Christians, because those who fall into this way of thinking find it challenging to acknowledge that they have committed the sin of self-righteousness.

Christians often use the term *self-righteousness* without considering its true meaning. Let me ask you a question: How would you define self-righteousness? Your answer might differ from mine or another Christian's. The most concise definition I have found is that a self-righteous person does not believe Christ's redemptive work on the cross is complete. Essentially, they view Jesus' payment for our sins as only a down payment, and they think that we must complete the payment through specific spiritual disciplines and religious works. This belief forms the foundation of religious tradition. However, Jesus warned His disciples that our traditions would render the Word of God powerless in our lives.

The Pharisee and the Tax Collector

Jesus taught a parable about the dangers of self-righteousness in Luke 18:9–14:

> Also He spoke this parable to some who trusted in themselves that they were righteous, and despised others: "Two men went up to the temple to pray, one a Pharisee and the other a tax collector. The Pharisee stood and prayed thus with himself, 'God, I thank You that I am not like other men—extortioners, unjust, adulterers, or even as this tax collector. I fast twice a week; I give tithes of all that I possess.' And the tax collector, standing afar off, would not so much as raise *his* eyes to heaven, but beat his breast, saying, 'God, be merciful to me a sinner!' I tell you, this man went down to his house justified *rather* than the other; for everyone who exalts himself will be humbled, and he who humbles himself will be exalted."

In this parable, Jesus describes two men who were praying in the temple. One was a Pharisee and the other a tax collector. Tax collectors were hated in that time and regarded by many as the worst type of sinner. They were Jews who were considered traitors because they worked for the Romans occupying Israel. As outcasts, they were often vindictive in their duties and considered to be deceitful. The Jewish people as a whole absolutely despised tax collectors, so the people listening to Jesus probably would not have been surprised by the Pharisee's attitude in the parable.

The Pharisee believed he was superior to the tax collector, and his prayer was full of pride regarding his religious position. Even though the Jewish people considered the tax collector to be in a low position, his prayer was humbler than the Pharisee's. He acknowledged his need for God's mercy and requested it earnestly. Many preachers have prayed like the Pharisee in this account. However, it is essential to remember that Jesus did not consider the Pharisee's prayer justified because it was full of self-righteousness. The tax collector's prayer, on the other hand, was humble and therefore justified.

Humility means relying on God. According to James 4:10, we must humble ourselves. God will not do this for us, but He will exalt those who do. The phrase "humble yourselves" in this verse is translated from the Greek word *tapeinoo*, which describes a person who has emptied themselves of their carnal ego and moved into a position of complete dependence on the Lord. In the next part of the verse, we see the words "in the sight of." The literal translation reads "in the presence of," which tells us that true humility can only be developed by purposefully spending time in the presence of God. You will find Him waiting to receive you if you commit to setting aside time each day to spend with Him.

Chapter 3

The Cross and the Power of God

For the message of the cross is foolishness to those who are perishing, but to us who are being saved it is the power of God.

1 CORINTHIANS 1:18

Throughout this book, I will make several references to "the message of the cross." Paul, too, mentioned the phrase in his letters, using it in two ways. Firstly, for nonbelievers, the idea of Jesus' being crucified and then resurrected seemed foolish. Crucifixion was a common form of capital punishment used by the Romans, and the damage inflicted on the physical body was well known. Unbelievers could not comprehend how a body that had gone through such horrors could still be in a condition to be raised from the dead.

Paul also refers to the cross as "the power of God" for a believer in 1 Corinthians 1:18. Christians should have a different perspective on the cross than those who do not believe. Rather than just seeing it as a symbol of the unimaginable suffering that Jesus endured, it is a gateway for us to enter the Christian life and experience the power and ability of God. The message of the cross encompasses not only Jesus' death but also His burial, descent into hell, and resurrection. Each of these events is an integral part of the redemption message.

The Religious Mindset

Another concept that I will be referring to is "the religious mindset." To explain this, let me share the childhood experience of a preacher I once met. He came from a family of pastors, evangelists, and missionaries. His father was an elder in their church, while his mother was the Sunday school superintendent. He shared stories with me of growing up in a family that valued their religious beliefs more than personal relationships. His parents enforced strict rules, such as prohibitions against playing cards, dancing, or wearing skirts. He and his siblings were raised to believe that God had high expectations, was easily angered, and was very difficult to please.

The preacher's parents enforced a religious mindset that implied God's blessings were given only to those who strictly followed religious disciplines. This meant they pursued God based on what they did to earn His favor. As a result, their children rebelled and stopped following religion, fearing that they would be punished with some disease or other terrible event for the slightest mistake. It was only when the preacher was in his thirties that he had a revelation of God's love and realized that God would accept him regardless of what he did in return. This revelation caused the preacher to serve God with even greater fervor than he had ever imagined possible.

Many Christians unknowingly fall into the traps set by religious spirits, which can lead them away from the message of the cross. To walk in true freedom and enjoy all Christ has provided, we must be aware of this danger. Satan, demons, and our unrenewed flesh all work together to push us away from God's grace and toward religious works. In my battle against this, I find it helpful to review Paul's words in Ephesians 1:7–12:

> In Him we have redemption through His blood, the forgiveness of sins, according to the riches of His grace

which He made to abound toward us in all wisdom and
prudence, having made known to us the mystery of His
will, according to His good pleasure which He purposed
in Himself, that in the dispensation of the fullness of
the times He might gather together in one all things
in Christ, both which are in heaven and which are on
earth—in Him. In Him also we have obtained an inheritance, being predestined according to the purpose of
Him who works all things according to the counsel of
His will, that we who first trusted in Christ should be
to the praise of His glory.

In the text, Paul doesn't use future tense. Instead, he says "we
have redemption through His blood" and "the forgiveness of sins"—
both in the present tense. We already have these things, and they're
not something we have to wait for. They're already provided to us
through God's grace. There's no mention of us earning redemption
or forgiveness through our own efforts. In fact, everything we need
has already been provided to us through Christ's redemptive work
on the cross. As I've mentioned before, we can't increase or decrease
the amount of grace given to us.

Freedom from Condemnation

To achieve freedom from the religious mindset, it is essential to first
acknowledge the sacrifice made by Jesus on the cross to pay for our
sins. This is why I believe that developing a revelation of the cross
is necessary to break free of religious thinking. Jesus gave up his life
to pay the debt we owed, which opened the door to God's presence
through his death, burial, and resurrection.

Over the years, I have come across many ideas on increasing
humility in our lives that focused on things we can do. However, I

believe that true humility can only be attained by recognizing the importance of the cross. As we gain a deeper understanding of the cross, our dependence on Jesus grows. We can only find freedom from condemnation by placing our complete trust in Jesus instead of relying on our own actions.

A truly humble individual is someone who looks to Jesus as the source of their strength in every aspect of life. James encouraged his readers to "humble yourselves in the sight of the Lord" (James 4:10). The phrase *humble yourselves* refers to the process of becoming entirely reliant on the Lord. We can achieve this by being present before Him. Spending more and more time in the Lord's presence will lead to a greater dependence on Him.

Many individuals who feel condemned, unworthy, or unfit for God's service are failing to put their faith in the message of the cross. Only by looking at the cross can we understand the atonement made by Jesus for humanity. Unfortunately, many people in today's church suffer from condemnation. Why is this? Our attention has shifted from the cross to more glamorous topics such as prosperity, healing, and revival. However, we must realize that it is solely through Christ's redemptive work on the cross that we can attain true prosperity, healing, and revival.

The Message of the Cross and the Gospel of Christ

A clearer comparison can be made by examining 1 Corinthians 1:18 and Romans 1:16.

> For the message of the cross is foolishness to those who are perishing, but to us who are being saved it is the power of God. (1 Corinthians 1:18)

> For I am not ashamed of the gospel of Christ, for it is the power of God to salvation for everyone who believes, for the Jew first and also for the Greek. (Romans 1:16)

These verses convey the message of the cross and the gospel of Christ. Though they are distinct, they are interconnected by Paul, who links God's power to both. It is impossible to preach the gospel of Christ without preaching the message of the cross, and vice versa. In Mark 16:20, it is said that the Lord works with those who preach His Word, and He will confirm the message that has been ministered. If we do not experience any accompanying manifestations of power, it may indicate that we are not preaching the gospel correctly or that it is not being received. Therefore, it is vital that we examine what we are teaching.

Jesus accomplished the work of redemption through His death, burial, and resurrection. After God raised Him from the dead, He ascended to heaven and is now seated at the right hand of God (Ephesians 1:20). As a result, we are called to enter into the rest that He has made available to us by paying the full price for our sins.

> For he who has entered His rest has himself also ceased from his works as God *did* from His. *Let us therefore be diligent to enter that rest,* lest anyone fall according to the same example of disobedience. (Hebrews 4:10–11, emphasis added in v. 11)

According to Ephesians 1:6, God can accept us by giving Jesus as a sacrifice on our behalf at the cross. The Christian life was never meant to be a constant pursuit of self-improvement. It is our religious tendencies that compel us to strive for the acceptance that we already have. Hebrews 4:16 tells us that we can confidently approach God's throne of grace because our acceptance is based on the cross and not our own efforts. Therefore, we can trust that God will always accept us when we approach His throne.

The Satanic Kingdom

The goal of a religious spirit is to divert our attention toward ourselves instead of Jesus. Such spirits employ various tactics to distract us, such as inducing sickness, creating a sense of lack, or exploiting social media. While there are numerous other distractions, the underlying point is that a person who is fixated on themselves cannot fully concentrate on Jesus. As a result, it becomes impossible to experience the complete provision of God in this situation.

The reason the cross was necessary is because no human being could save themselves from being under Satan's control. When God created Adam, He gave him complete authority over the earth. Adam was like a "god" (with a little *g*) of this world. However, when he and his wife ate fruit from the only tree on Earth that God had told them not to eat from, they handed over the keys of the physical realm to Satan. This resulted in Satan's becoming the god (with a little *g*) of this world, as we see in 2 Corinthians 4:4.

Religious spirits operate in the physical realm. Our relationship with God is in the spiritual realm. We communicate with Him spirit to spirit, and it is only through the cross of Christ that this is made possible. The distractions used by these spirits are meant to turn our attention toward the natural realm and away from the spiritual. Paul tells us in Romans 8:5 that "those who live according to the flesh set their minds on the things of the flesh." These are the people who have allowed themselves to become distracted and live a "carnal" life that is dominated by the carnal mind.

According to the Bible, Satan was not given authority over the physical realm indefinitely. In the King James Version of 2 Corinthians

4:4, the word *world* should be more accurately translated as "age," as it is in the New King James Version of the Bible. We are currently living in what is referred to as "the last days," as there are enough prophetic events taking place to suggest that the end of this age is near, and we are likely to witness it at the time of Christ's return. This event is commonly known as the rapture. Following this event, there will be a seven-year tribulation period, which is described in several books of the Bible. At the end of the seven years, Jesus will return once more to establish His kingdom on Earth, and Satan will be thrown into the lake of fire forever after being bound for a thousand years (Revelation 20).

The Debt Has Been Paid

The message of the cross is the good news this world is seeking. It tells us that God did not wait until humanity could earn His love. Instead, He recognized our hopeless condition and sent Jesus to reconcile us with no strings attached. It's important to emphasize that God sent Jesus without any expectations from us because many people think that they must earn His love. They have become exhausted in their pursuit of His acceptance, which was given in Christ Jesus before they were born again. In Ephesians 1:3–11, Paul lists several spiritual benefits that have already been given to us, including being accepted by God, being adopted into His family, and being forgiven for our sins. We see in Romans 10:10 that the only requirement set for anyone to access these benefits is to believe in their heart and confess Jesus as Lord. It really is that simple.

According to 2 Corinthians 4:4, Satan is the "god" of this world. When we were born, we automatically become his subjects due to the sin nature that is passed down to us from Adam and Eve. However, Romans 5:10 tells us that God reconciled us to Himself through the death of Christ on the cross, even before we were born and had the chance to sin. The term *reconcile* refers to a decisive change that brings two people into a relationship. Although we were once subjects of the satanic kingdom, which is an enemy of God, it did not stop God from sending Jesus to the cross to reconcile us to Himself.

The sin committed by Adam and Eve had devastating consequences that continue to impact humanity. As their descendants, we have all inherited the sin nature that was passed down to us. The cost of sin is death, as stated in Romans 6:23. This left no other option for God but to redeem humanity. He sent Jesus to the cross to pay the price for all of us with His death. As Paul explains in Colossians 2:13, Jesus' death wiped out the requirements that were against us, and he also nailed the note showing it was due to the cross. This means that Jesus not only paid the debt, but he also erased the evidence of it.

How did Jesus pay the price for our sins with His death? The answer to this question is found in 2 Corinthians 5:21 which tells us God "made Him who knew no sin to be sin for us, that we might become the righteousness of God in Him." This is an amazing verse. The sin of every person for all time was placed on Jesus at the cross, and in His death, He satisfied the requirements to appease God's wrath against humanity. Many people struggle with religious traditions that warn them about doing anything that could cause God to become angry with them. I experienced this struggle firsthand while growing up due to the teachings of the church my family attended. Words cannot begin to express the freedom I experienced when the Holy Spirit imparted this revelation that Jesus appeased all of God's wrath.

Jesus Paid the Full Price for Our Sins

Many religious traditions emphasize our outward actions, which are believed to earn God's favor. Unfortunately, this has led many well-meaning Christians to falsely believe that they must perform certain actions to achieve righteousness. This has, in turn, led many people to extreme measures in their pursuit for God's acceptance. For example, there are accounts of people allowing themselves to be nailed to a cross or crawling for miles over broken glass as penance for their sins. However, these actions are a rejection of Christ's redemptive work, which they may not realize. Such extreme measures reflect a lack of understanding of the message of the cross.

I often wonder how many of us who identify as Christians have taken the time to reflect on the significance of the cross. I personally didn't give it much thought during my early years of serving God. Many people tend to believe that Christ's death was only meant to provide for the forgiveness of our sins. This is why so many people struggle to develop a deep relationship with God, often resorting to extreme measures in an attempt to earn God's acceptance.

To experience the freedom that God intends for you, it is essential to understand that Jesus has fulfilled the requirements of heaven's justice system. There was a cost to be paid for our sins, and Jesus paid that price by His death, burial, and resurrection. No amount of good deeds, religious rituals, or Christian service projects can achieve what the Lord accomplished for us on the cross. Our religious actions will not earn God's forgiveness or elevate our status with Him. Our entire relationship with God is based solely on the cross.

Chapter 4

The Price Jesus Paid

Let this mind be in you which was also in Christ Jesus, who, being
in the form of God, did not consider it robbery to be equal with God,
but made Himself of no reputation, taking the form of a bondservant,
and coming in the likeness of men. And being found in appearance
as a man, He humbled Himself and became obedient to the point
of death, even the death of the cross. Therefore God also has highly
exalted Him and given Him the name which is above every name.

PHILIPPIANS 2:5–9

A pastor once shared a story about his son who asked if he could see an R-rated movie with his friends. The father inquired about the movie's rating, and his son said that it was rated R, but only because of some profanity and nudity. The son assured his father that the rest of the movie was good. However, the father refused to let his son go, and the son tried to argue but failed. The father suggested that his son invite his friends for a sleepover to make up for it the following weekend. The friends came over and were playing when the father entered the room with a fresh batch of brownies he had just baked. As the boys each excitedly took a plate, he warned them that there was a small amount of dog poop in the brownies but that it would not affect the flavor. The boys were disgusted and refused to eat them, even after the father tried to assure them that it was just a very small amount of poop and wouldn't make them sick. They still refused to eat the brownies. The father got his message across, and his son never asked him to see an R-rated movie again.

Psalm 23:5 speaks of how God has set a table for us, even when we are in the presence of our enemies. This table was prepared at the cross, and in the previous chapter, we learned how our own self-centered works pale in comparison to what Jesus did for us through his death, burial, and resurrection. God doesn't require us to do anything to earn our place at the table. Instead, we only need to sit down and enjoy the goodness that God has already provided for us. The meal is cooked, the table settings have been placed, and the drinks have been poured. Any effort to earn our way to the table is like the figurative poop in the story of the brownies. It only hinders us from enjoying what God has already prepared for us.

Our Self-Righteousness Renders the Word of God Powerless in Our Lives

Jesus warned His disciples that our traditions can make the Word of God ineffective (Mark 7:13). Such traditions often stem from self-righteous approaches to the message of the cross. This can lead to a false idea that Jesus only made a partial payment for our sins and that we need to work off the remaining balance through religious works and service. However, this notion is entirely untrue. Jesus paid the total price for our sins, and as a result, He opened the door for us to enter a personal relationship with our heavenly Father.

I have previously mentioned that the main reason for our struggles in our Christian journey is our lack of understanding about the price that Jesus paid to redeem us. This understanding cannot be obtained through our natural abilities. In 1 Corinthians 2:7, Paul discusses the "hidden *wisdom* which God ordained before the ages for our glory." This wisdom can only be revealed to those who are willing to dedicate time to meditating on the truths of God's Word. The

Holy Spirit was sent by God to reveal this wisdom to us (1 Corinthians 2:10). I believe that the core revelation He will impart to our hearts is that of the cross of Christ.

James teaches us the importance of humbling ourselves before the Lord (James 4:10). Humbling ourselves means relying entirely on God. But how can we achieve this? James explains that we need to spend time with God in prayer and read His Word. As we do so, we will find ourselves becoming more and more dependent on Him. However, our self-righteous works can hinder this process by shifting our focus from Jesus to ourselves. We are not truly looking at the cross if we attempt to earn God's favor through our own efforts.

Jesus Suffered for You

Let's take a moment to reflect on the immense physical pain that Jesus endured on the cross. It is my belief that His suffering is beyond the comprehension of our natural minds. Only through the wisdom imparted by the Holy Spirit can we begin to understand what happened at the cross. His sufferings went beyond the physical realm. Paul tells us that God even made Jesus to be sin so that we could receive His righteousness. It's hard to imagine the Son of God being made sin. I don't think any of us can even begin to fathom the depth of love expressed by God in His willingness to do this.

In Isaiah 53, there is a description of Jesus' suffering that can be difficult to understand. Verse 10 states that it "pleased the LORD to bruise Him," which is a remarkable statement. I believe that God sent Jesus to the cross because He knew it was the only way to pay the price for humanity's sin. This is why I mentioned in the Introduction that the cross was a beautiful expression of God's love for us. Despite unimaginable suffering, Jesus endured it all to restore our fellowship with God.

God Became a Man

Jesus paid a huge price to save humanity. He started His journey by being born of a virgin, which required Him to make "Himself of no reputation, taking the form of a bondservant" (Philippians 2:7). It can be challenging for us to fully understand the significance of this sacrifice. To put it in perspective, let's consider the following description of God from Isaiah 40:12:

> Who has measured the waters in the hollow of His hand, measured heaven with a span and calculated the dust of the earth in a measure? Weighed the mountains in scales and the hills in a balance?

As I read this verse, I couldn't help but wonder how God, who is capable of measuring heaven with His hand, chose to limit Himself to a human body. Although it seems impossible, that is exactly what Jesus did. The concept of someone as great and vast as God doing something like this is almost mind-boggling.

The Bible contains numerous verses like Isaiah 40:12 that depict the vastness of our God. It is beneficial to spend some time reflecting on them to put the extent of His sacrifice for us into context. We read in John 1:1–5 that God made everything using His Word. Verse 14 tells us that the Word of God became flesh. This is a reference to Jesus setting aside His divinity to become a man. The cost that Jesus paid started with His birth as a human when He restricted Himself to a physical body. Consider this in conjunction with Psalm 33:6, which tells us: "By the word of the LORD the heavens were made, and all the host of them by the breath of His mouth." That means every star we can see in the night sky originated with the Word of God, who came to the earth, limited Himself to a human body, and then allowed Himself to be crucified by people He had created.

Jesus Was Rejected

God created everything by speaking His Word. This means that the sun, moon, and stars we see in the sky were all brought into existence by His mouth. While it is difficult to imagine, it is even harder for me to think of such a powerful God limiting Himself to a human body. However, this is precisely what Jesus did. He is the Word of God who came to this earth through a virgin birth for the sole purpose of setting events into motion that would ultimately lead to Him hanging on a cross to pay the price for humanity's sin.

The Word of God chose to limit Himself in a human body and walked the earth for just over thirty-three years. During His time among us, He interacted with people who had no idea they had encountered their creator. Although some experienced the power of God flowing through His ministry, only a few had any level of revelation regarding His identity. Even His disciples, who had forsaken everything to follow Him, struggled to fully embrace Jesus' divine identity.

Numerous books have been authored by people who have died and visited heaven. Jesus is revered and celebrated in heaven, but on Earth He has been rejected by the majority of people since the time of His ministry. Even during His earthly ministry, He was rejected by the Jewish people, opening the door for His crucifixion. Although a few recognized Him as their Messiah, most did not. It is difficult to fathom that the Son of God grew up as a human child amidst people who were unaware that He was their creator. To them, Jesus was just another ordinary boy growing up in their town.

Chapter 5

What Are We Looking At?

For He shall grow up before Him as a tender plant,
And as a root out of dry ground.
He has no form or comeliness;
And when we see Him,
There is no beauty that we should desire Him.
He is despised and rejected by men,
A Man of sorrows and acquainted with grief.
And we hid, as it were, our faces from Him;
He was despised, and we did not esteem Him.

ISAIAH 53:2–3

The magnitude of Jesus' sacrifice is beyond our natural understanding. We need the guidance of the Holy Spirit to fully comprehend it. Jesus chose to humbly relinquish His divinity and take on human form. Isaiah described Him as an ordinary man with no physical features that set Him apart from others. This means that if you passed Jesus on the street, you would not have noticed anything remarkable about Him. There is no evidence in Scripture or historical records that Jesus did anything to promote Himself.

Jesus possessed the ability to make people believe in Him without a doubt. He could have revealed Himself in all His glory, proving His divinity. However, Jesus chose not to do so. Instead, He decided to remain in a physical body for eternity. Jesus is still embodied, but in a glorified form. Unlike the Father and the Holy Spirit, who do not have physical bodies, Jesus was a spirit who chose to become a man and identify with humanity for all eternity. He did this to provide us with a way of being reconciled with our heavenly Father.

The Power of the Gospel

Jesus chose to relinquish His divinity and become a human being (Philippians 2:5–8) to pay the penalty for our sins. His work is finished. However, some individuals may believe that they are unworthy to approach God's throne, or they question if God will answer their prayers. This is because they lack the realization of their identity in Christ, which has negated the message of the cross and its power in their lives. Rather than requesting an outpouring of the Spirit, praying for a renewed understanding of who we are in Christ Jesus would be much more beneficial.

The power of the gospel lies in what Christ accomplished for us through His death, burial, and resurrection. It is not dependent on our actions in this life. Although living a holy life is important, our holiness only responds to what Christ did for us. Our good deeds will not force God to act or answer our prayers. Contrary to some teachings today, our goodness or good works do not determine whether our prayers will be answered. God answers our prayers solely based on our faith in the name of Jesus.

It is only through faith that we can experience the power of God. I have discussed the operation of faith in detail in my book *Walking in the Faith of the Son of God*. Understanding that God's power cannot flow through a person not operating in faith is important. Many people have attempted to tap into this power but fail because they have yet to realize this fact. It is like trying to turn on an electric lamp without plugging it in. The lamp will not work without a connection to the source, which can only be established by plugging it into an electrical outlet.

It's essential to engage with His Word and the Holy Spirit daily to connect with God's power. If we neglect to do so, we may become distracted by our desires rather than focused on following the path He has for us. We put ourselves in His place when we believe that we must earn God's favor through religious activities like attending church or fasting. Instead, we should remain humble and focus on our relationship with Him rather than trying to earn His approval through our actions.

I have heard some ministers say that for God to work in our lives, we must engage in religious works. However, I believe this is a misinterpretation of the gospel. This belief has caused many people to miss out on the benefits of Christ's sacrifice on the cross. Even Paul warned the Galatians that their dependence on their own works could cause them to become estranged from Christ (Galatians 5:4). The term *estranged* can also mean "forfeit," "fade away," or "become fruitless." In other words, it describes a situation where we have fallen from grace. This does not mean we have lost our salvation. Instead of relying on Christ's redemptive work, we rely on our righteousness and goodness. This is like the story I shared in the previous chapter about the pastor who said he had added dog poop to the brownies. It only takes a small amount to ruin the whole thing!

Turning Our Attention toward Christ

T. L. Osborn was a minister who was renowned for the miraculous works that occurred in his meetings. He had one primary goal in ministry: to shift people's focus away from himself and the religious traditions they may have been taught. Dr. Osborn believed that by doing so, the people's attention could be directed toward Jesus as the only true healer. He discovered that miracles would begin to flow when people centered their attention solely on Jesus and His death, burial, and resurrection. Thousands of people would be healed during his meetings, and this was only possible because he learned to turn their attention toward Jesus.

It is rare to find ministries like T. L. Osborn's nowadays. Although some operate in the miraculous, most of them focus on emotionally uplifting people to prepare them for receiving a miracle. The emphasis is on an emotional experience rather than on Christ. It is common to hear services advertised as times of impartation or outflowing of the double portion. However, it is unclear what the double portion is since every Christian already has the Holy Spirit living inside of their born-again spirit.

I used to be a member of a church that put a lot of emphasis on emotionally driven experiences during services. Although some people were blessed with miraculous healings, most left the services feeling disappointed. The ministers almost always blamed the congregation for their lack of faith and never took responsibility for their actions. However, while ministering in a small country church one Sunday, my perspective changed completely. The Holy Spirit spoke to me, urging me to focus on Him rather than His gifts of healing and miracles. During the service, a lady in a wheelchair arrived and became more and more eager to connect with the Holy Spirit as she listened to me talk about Him. In the middle of the message, she jumped out of her wheelchair and ran to the altar area, asking me to introduce her to the Holy Spirit. Much later in the service, the pastor and I realized she had been miraculously healed. The congregation immediately noticed it, and people shouted and praised the Lord! The key lesson here is that by shifting our focus to the person of the Holy Spirit and the relationship He desires to have with each of us, miracles can still occur without needing an emotionally driven atmosphere.

Chapter 6

Free from the Bondage of Sin

For the law, having a shadow of the good things to come, and *not the very image of the things, can never with these same sacrifices, which they offer continually year by year, make those who approach perfect. For then would they not have ceased to be offered? For the worshipers, once purified, would have had no more consciousness of sins. But in those* sacrifices there is *a reminder of sins every year. For it is not possible that the blood of bulls and goats could take away sins.*

HEBREWS 10:1–4

My wife and I used to attend a church that emphasized faith in its teachings. Almost every service revolved around messages centered on faith, healing, and prosperity. One would think that with such an emphasis on faith, every person attending the church would experience miracles. However, the sad truth was that most members struggled just like those who had never heard this message. Most of the congregation would respond when the pastor called for an altar prayer for the sick. Surprisingly, even the church staff members would head forward for prayer. I was always amazed to sit in those services, watching people head to the altar, hoping to receive something from God.

Why do you think we don't see more miraculous demonstrations today? Every Christian has a different opinion of the answer to this question. Since Jesus hasn't changed, the problem must be on our side. We are the ones who hinder the flow of miracles. One reason for this could be the mentality that only our ministers are anointed, which has created a culture where only specific individuals are believed to have the power to impart healing. However, this belief contradicts the Word of God, which makes it clear that every Christian is anointed by the Holy Spirit, who lives in their spirit.

Holiness Is a Byproduct of Our Relationship with God

I am constantly amazed by God's immense love for all of us. This unconditional love cannot be increased or decreased by anything we do. When we genuinely understand this love, we naturally strive toward living a holy life. However, many people fall into the trap of trying to earn God's love, even though it has already been freely given. The Holy Spirit taught me one of the most profound lessons several years ago: Holiness is the byproduct of our relationship with God. It is not a means to attain a relationship, as some may teach.

Holiness is an essential aspect of our relationship with God. While some ministers may argue otherwise, it helps us maintain a sensitive heart toward Him. However, it's important to understand that striving for holiness doesn't automatically earn us God's affection and love. He loved us even before we were worthy of His love, and He doesn't expect us to cleanse ourselves before accepting us. It's important to remember that we must always place our dependence on Him, even after we have purified ourselves.

I have noticed that people who have a hard time living a holy life need an understanding of the significance of the cross. When we forget what Jesus accomplished on the cross, we become vulnerable to the attacks of the devil. Since the devil can't criticize or accuse Jesus, he turns his attention toward us instead. But, if we focus on the cross and recognize its power, the devil will have no power to condemn us. This is because Jesus paid the price for our sins; all we need to do is have faith in Him. Anyone who fully understands this truth will not struggle with feelings of condemnation.

The Cross and the Gospel

For I am not ashamed of the gospel of Christ, for it is the power of God to salvation for everyone who believes, for the Jew first and also for the Greek. (Romans 1:16)

The Greek word for *salvation* has a broader meaning than just the forgiveness of sins. It also includes healing, prosperity, and deliverance, which are all aspects of Jesus' mission. Therefore, the power of God to grant us salvation in the form of forgiveness of sins, healing, prosperity, and deliverance is revealed through the gospel, which is the amazing news of Jesus Christ.

The church as a whole isn't preaching the right message. Instead of telling people the good news of the gospel, we often focus on telling them that they're sinners and that they're going to hell because of their sins. While it's true that we were all sinners before we were born again, this isn't the whole truth of the gospel. This message only brings condemnation, not hope. We should focus on sharing the good news of God's love and grace and how we can be reconciled to Him through Jesus Christ.

The gospel teaches us that God placed all the punishment for our sins on Jesus. Despite our sins, unworthiness, and need, Christ paid the price for us. Justice demanded our punishment, but Jesus took it for us. As a result, God's wrath has been forever satisfied, and He is not angry with us anymore. Jesus paid the price; all we need to do is accept that payment. This is good news—this is the gospel!

Help in a Time of Need

I have heard some ministers speak about confessing every sin before we pray. Some even suggest that God won't accept our prayers because we need forgiveness first. However, they miss Hebrews 4:16, which tells us to approach God boldly "in time of need." The Greek word translated as "need" refers to a critical need for urgent assistance. God has provided a solution for every issue through the cross and desires us to approach Him whenever we encounter trouble. This is a much different picture of God than what many Christians believe.

The cross has made provision for all our needs, thanks to Jesus paying the price. Imagine walking into a store and finding out that someone has already paid for every item in it. You can take anything off the shelves because it's already been paid for, and the salesclerks won't stop you. Wouldn't you feel confident and bold walking into that store? I sure would!

According to Peter, God has already given us everything we need to live a godly life (2 Peter 1:3). We need to have knowledge of Him. Unfortunately, our ignorance of the cross prevents us from accessing what is rightfully ours. Thankfully, the Holy Spirit is here to teach us and reveal the knowledge we need to use all that has been provided. All we have to do is acknowledge that He is already living within us and waiting for an invitation to guide us.

The Bible says that Jesus has provided us with an eternal redemption that has paid the price for every sin (Hebrews 9:11–12). It's important to note that we don't have to do anything to earn God's love, grace, or favor. Christ has already done the work, and our only expectation is to rest in Him. However, this doesn't mean that we won't face any trials or battles. We will certainly have an adversary, but we should approach every situation from a position of victory rather than one focused on obtaining victory. This is a different perspective than what most Christians have.

Jesus Paid Our Bill

Romans 5:13 states that "sin is not imputed when there is no law." The word *impute* is not commonly used in everyday language. It is a term used in accounting that you may not be familiar with. To better understand it, let's consider a credit card. When you use a credit card to pay for something at a store, you are not actually paying for the item at that moment. If you think otherwise, tell your credit card company you have already paid the merchant when you receive your monthly bill!

When you use a credit card to pay for goods at a store, the credit card machine at the register collects information about your credit card company and sends the charge to them. The merchant uses this information to impute the cost of the goods being purchased to your account. However, you don't actually pay for the goods at the time of purchase. Instead, your credit card company sends out a monthly bill for the charges, which you will have to pay later.

If I were to walk up to the register and put my credit card in the machine while you were checking out, the cost of your goods would be charged to my account. You wouldn't have to pay anything, as my credit card company would send me the bill. However, I wouldn't receive any benefit, since you took the goods home even though I paid for them. The merchant wouldn't expect anything from you, since they didn't receive your credit card information.

Imagine if you went to a store and bought some goods using a credit card, but the bill was never sent to you. Instead, it was sent to the credit card company and they paid for it on your behalf. This is similar to what Jesus did for us; he paid for our sins on the cross, and we get to enjoy the benefits of this redemption without owing anything. Many Christians fail to appreciate this fact and forget to thank Jesus for paying the bill we owed with His life.

Chapter 7

The Great Exchange

But now the righteousness of God apart from the law is revealed, being witnessed by the Law and the Prophets, even the righteousness of God, through faith in Jesus Christ, to all and on all who believe. For there is no difference; for all have sinned and fall short of the glory of God, being justified freely by His grace through the redemption that is in Christ Jesus, whom God set forth as a propitiation by His blood, through faith, to demonstrate His righteousness, because in His forbearance God had passed over the sins that were previously committed, to demonstrate at the present time His righteousness, that He might be just and the justifier of the one who has faith in Jesus.

ROMANS 3:21–26

Jesus paid the ultimate price for all of our sins and unrighteousness on the cross. Through His death, He redeemed us. According to Isaiah 40:2, Jesus didn't just pay for our sins once, but twice. This is like paying $200 to a cashier for a $100 charge, and God allowed this to happen so that Satan could not challenge our redemption. The price has already been paid twice, and we don't need to do anything except accept what has been provided to us in Christ Jesus through His faith.

On the cross, Jesus paid for our sins because we were unable to pay the debt ourselves. As we learned in the previous chapter, the price we owed was "imputed" to His account. However, Jesus did not stop there. He paid the price for our debt and gifted us with His righteousness. This gift is something that we could never earn or deserve. It is an insult to the cross when we walk around with a consciousness of sin that denies what Christ accomplished for us.

The Great Exchange

I like to think of the cross as the place where Jesus made the ultimate exchange. He made the ultimate sacrifice by taking on all our sins and giving us His righteousness instead. This is what makes the gospel such good news. Jesus has enabled us to receive His righteousness by paying the total price for our sins. However, many Christians today are still living in bondage to their sins because they have not been told that Jesus has already paid the price for them. Jesus has opened the door for us to walk free, and we should embrace this freedom provided to us in the cross.

The core message of Christianity is that Jesus has paid the price for our sins. It is important to spread this simple truth far and wide. For instance, many people who are struggling with illnesses and diseases are unaware that Jesus has already taken their sufferings upon Himself and bore them on the cross. This is mentioned in 1 Peter 2:24. Instead of endlessly searching for a cure, people should trust in Jesus and receive the healing that He has already made available to them. All they need to do is have faith.

I ministered to people who found it hard to accept the blessings made available to them through Jesus' sacrifice on the cross. They felt unworthy of receiving anything from God, believing they did not deserve it. Their eyes were on themselves and what they thought they deserved. However, the truth is that no one who has accepted Jesus as their Lord and Savior will receive what they truly deserve. We are all undeserving of salvation, healing, and freedom from condemnation. Anyone who feels otherwise is being self-righteous and needs to address this attitude. Otherwise, they will continue to miss out on all the wonderful things God has provided us through Christ.

Our Worth Is Found in the Cross

We do not deserve anything from God. It is only because of the cross that we can receive anything from Him. Jesus paid the price of our debt through His death, burial, and resurrection. The Lord was "made" sin by God on the cross so that we could be "made" righteous." (2 Corinthians 5:21). Without the cross, every human being would be condemned to eternal separation from God. This is why the message of the cross is such great news.

If someone believes they can earn God's approval through their actions and righteousness, they have embraced the Law. However, the Law alone cannot save anyone, so the cross is essential. In Galatians 5:4, Paul explains that anyone who tries to justify themselves before God based on their good works has "fallen from grace." In this context, the Greek word translated as "fallen" means to drift off course from the straight path.

There is a lesser-known aspect to the message of the cross that is often overlooked. We all know that being self-righteous and following religious traditions renders the power of the cross ineffective, as stated in 1 Corinthians 1:17. However, the reverse is also true: When we truly comprehend the message of the cross, self-righteousness, condemnation, and religious traditions become powerless in our lives. When we gain a revelation of the message of the cross, we are equipped to live a holy life and become more sensitive to God. It is important to note that living a holy life does not make God more sensitive to us. Our standing with God is based solely on what Jesus achieved on the cross, and our natural human efforts cannot change the way He views us.

Persecution and the
Message of the Cross

Romans 1:16 states that the "gospel of Christ" has the power of God for salvation. This verse is commonly referenced in sermons. However, it is often overlooked that the cross is the power of the gospel, as stated in 1 Corinthians 1:18. The message of the cross is the gospel of Christ. Without the cross, there would be no gospel!

Paul speaks in Galatians 6:12–15 of persecution that arises from preaching the "cross of Christ," and he emphasizes the need to boast only "in the cross of our Lord Jesus Christ."

> As many as desire to make a good showing in the flesh, these *would* compel you to be circumcised, only that they may not suffer persecution for the cross of Christ. For not even those who are circumcised keep the law, but they desire to have you circumcised that they may boast in your flesh. *But God forbid that I should boast except in the cross of our Lord Jesus Christ,* by whom the world has been crucified to me, and I to the world. For in Christ Jesus neither circumcision nor uncircumcision avails anything, but a new creation. (Emphasis added in v. 14)

The one who preaches the message of Christ's crucifixion will face persecution. Any form of persecution is centered around this message alone. There is no middle ground in this area. Religious teachings often focus on personal efforts. They make people believe that God will not be willing to bless them unless they start living a holy life. This message is widely accepted in religious circles but is not true to the gospel message. In a sense, it can be seen as a reflection of the saying that we only get what we deserve, which is entirely opposite to the true message of the gospel.

We must have spiritual discernment to understand that everything we receive through the cross is a gift from our Lord Jesus. However, the religious mindset often opposes this idea. Instead, it emphasizes our goodness and self-effort, which becomes irrelevant if everything is given to us as a gift. The message of the cross removes any sense of self-righteousness by focusing all attention on Jesus alone.

The End of Boasting

Martin Luther rediscovered the message of salvation through faith alone. The concepts we have been discussing in this chapter transformed his life. His journey into the message of the cross began with Romans 3:27:

> Where *is* boasting then? It is excluded. By what law? Of works? No, but by the law of faith.

The Holy Spirit played a crucial role in Martin Luther's life by using Romans 3:27 to change the course of his journey and lead him to become the founder of the Protestant Reformation. Luther believed that this verse was a divine revelation given to him by the Spirit. Over the years, I have spent a considerable amount of time contemplating this verse. It teaches us that we should always place our trust in Christ's finished work alone, eliminating any opportunity to boast about our own efforts.

The message of the cross is central to Paul's statement in Romans 3:27. If someone understands this message, they cannot boast about their accomplishments. Instead, they become entirely reliant on Christ. Any good deeds they perform stem from first humbling themselves before Jesus and accepting His gift of salvation.

In our Christian journey, everything revolves around Jesus. He is the reason behind all our successes and any positive happenings in our lives. When someone promotes themselves, it shows that they don't comprehend the true meaning of the cross. Unfortunately, it's quite common in Christian circles to see individuals being glorified more than Christ. To experience God's power more in our lives, we need to let go of the Christian celebrity mindset. Every Christian is equal in the eyes of God because He views us through Christ Jesus.

So, it is important not to boast about anything except the cross, as Jesus has already paid the price and completed the work. When standing before Him, you will not be required to present your achievements resume from this life. Through my experiences, I have caught a glimpse of the glory of God over the years, which has helped me realize how entirely dependent I am on the cross. This realization will also help you understand the same and set you on the path toward a life filled with the power of God, moving through you to the dark and dying world around you.

Chapter 8

Are You Now Being Made Perfect by the Flesh?

*O foolish Galatians! Who has bewitched you that you should
not obey the truth, before whose eyes Jesus Christ was clearly
portrayed among you as crucified? This only I want to learn
from you: Did you receive the Spirit by the works of the law, or
by the hearing of faith? Are you so foolish? Having begun in the
Spirit, are you now being made perfect by the flesh? Have you
suffered so many things in vain—if indeed it was in vain?*

GALATIANS 3:1–4

Paul did not intend to be politically correct when he wrote these
words. The Greek word translated as "foolish" in this verse refers
to a person behaving mindlessly and densely, not using reason to
think through a matter. Imagine receiving a letter addressed to you
in such a manner. This type of language would not be tolerated in
the church today and would likely be met with criticism.

The J. B. Phillips translation of Galatians 3:1–5 reads:

O you dear idiots of Galatia, who saw Jesus Christ the
crucified so plainly, who has been casting a spell over you?
I will ask you one simple question: did you receive the
Spirit of God by trying to keep the Law or by believing

57

the message of the Gospel? Surely you can't be so idiotic as to think that a man begins his spiritual life in the Spirit and then completes it by reverting to outward observances? Has all your painful experience brought you nowhere? I simply cannot believe it of you! Does God, who gives you his Spirit and works miracles among you, do these things because you have obeyed the Law or because you have believed the Gospel? Ask yourselves that.

The Amplified Bible, Classic Edition of Galatians 3:1 reads:

O you poor *and* silly *and* thoughtless *and* unreflecting *and* senseless Galatians! Who has fascinated *or* bewitched *or* cast a spell over you, unto whom—right before your very eyes—Jesus Christ (the Messiah) was openly *and* graphically set forth *and* portrayed as crucified?

Finally, The Message translation of Galatians 3:1 reads:

You crazy Galatians! Did someone put a spell on you? Have you taken leave of your senses? Something crazy has happened, for it's obvious that you no longer have the crucified Jesus in clear focus in your lives. His sacrifice on the cross was certainly set before you clearly enough.

Paul's letters do not hold back on criticism where it is necessary. In one verse, he refers to his readers as poor, silly, thoughtless, crazy, senseless, and idiots. This sentiment is consistent in both the books of Galatians and Romans, but the tone differs. While Romans takes a more scholarly approach, Galatians conveys a sense of Paul's anger toward the believers in Galatia, as evidenced by the various translations of Galatians 3:1–5.

Grace and the Gospel

One example of Paul's frustration with the Galatian believers is found in Galatians 1:6:

> I marvel that you are turning away so soon from Him
> who called you in the grace of Christ, to a different gospel.

Paul uses the terms *gospel* and *grace of Christ* interchangeably. It's interesting to note that every promise of God is made available to us through His grace. It's important to understand that anyone who preaches a performance-based gospel is not preaching the gospel of Christ. The gospel is the power of God unto salvation (Romans 1:16).

Let's reconsider 1 Corinthians 1:18 in light of our discussion on *grace* and *the gospel* being used interchangeably in Paul's letters:

> For the message of the cross is foolishness to those who
> are perishing, but to us who are being saved it is the
> power of God.

The message of the cross is the message of grace, and anyone teaching the gospel must emphasize this truth. Unfortunately, many churches today do not prioritize the completed work of Christ on the cross; instead, they place too much emphasis on our own works. As a result, God's power may not manifest in the way it should. One common belief that has no scriptural basis is that we are saved by grace but must maintain our salvation through works. Sprinkling bits and pieces of grace into our messages is not enough; we must focus on the grace of God above all else.

The Corrupted Gospel

Paul warns us in Galatians 1:7 of those who want to distort the gospel:

> There are some who trouble you and want to pervert the
> gospel of Christ.

The word translated as "pervert" in this verse refers to altering or corrupting the message of the gospel. Sometimes this happens unintentionally, and people may not even realize they have done so. One common way this happens is when requirements such as good deeds, virtuous living, or regular church attendance are applied to earning God's approval. However, as we have already established, God's favor is given based on Christ's redemptive work accomplished on the cross alone.

Dealing with someone who openly denies Jesus is much easier than dealing with those who claim to believe in Him but add a "but" statement. For example, "Christ paid for my sins, but He still expects me to participate in communion to earn God's favor." These people acknowledge that Jesus was the Son of God and died on the cross, but then they add conditions such as, "You also have to..." This behavior is what Paul condemns in Galatians, as it perverts the true message of the cross, which has no "buts" in it.

Many ministers today are not preaching the complete gospel message. Instead, they are preaching a distorted version that leads people into the chains of condemnation. This has resulted in most Christians living under the burden of the same things that Christ died to set them free from. Only the pure gospel message can bring freedom from these weights.

Paul continues in Galatians 1:8–9 with some very harsh words for those who would corrupt the message of the cross:

> But even if we, or an angel from heaven, preach any other
> gospel to you than what we have preached to you, *let him*

be accursed. As we have said before, so now I say again, if anyone preaches any other gospel to you than what you have received, *let him be accursed.* (Emphasis added)

He used the phrase *let him be accursed* twice. This literally means "be damned to hell." I have heard ministers try to sugarcoat Paul's words with the claim that he did not really mean what he wrote. This is not surprising, as we tend to avoid any form of confrontation in churches today. What do you think? If he repeated himself, do you think he meant what he was writing? I sure do!

What Would Paul Say about Us?

After reading Paul's words in Galatians, and I can't help but wonder what he would think of the current state of the church. While there are some communities that preach the same message that he did, they seem to be scarce. If you've come this far in the book, it's obvious that you're not here to just get by. Your continued reading tells me that you're seeking the pure gospel message with a hunger in your heart.

We began this chapter with a quote from Galatians 3:1: "O foolish Galatians! Who has bewitched you?" At first glance, it may seem shocking that he would address his readers in this way. However, I believe that it was their behavior that prompted him to be so stern. As a former leader in the Jewish religion, he intimately understood the bondages that come with a works-based approach to God. Having heard reports, he probably could not believe that anyone would be willing to abandon the grace of God in favor of religious works.

The Holy Spirit Reveals the Crucifixion

Those who witnessed the crucifixion of Jesus did not possess the Holy Spirit, and thus, they lacked the ability to fully comprehend the significance of the events unfolding before them. However, as believers, we have the Holy Spirit dwelling within us, and He enables us to understand the profound meaning of Jesus' suffering in a way that transcends our physical senses.

The followers of Jesus who witnessed His crucifixion did not have the same understanding as we do today. Despite Jesus having previously told them that He could call forth legions of angels to assist Him, they did not fully comprehend this at the time. It is unlikely that any of them realized that the Lord could have called those angels and saved Himself from the cross if He so wished. However, He chose not to do so and selflessly gave His life to redeem us from our sins.

It must have felt like all hope was lost when Jesus was crucified. Those who witnessed it must have felt an overwhelming sense of despair. However, with the guidance of the Holy Spirit, we can understand that Jesus willingly sacrificed Himself. This was not something that those present could comprehend at the time. In Galatians 3:1, Paul makes reference to this revelation:

> Before whose eyes Jesus Christ was clearly portrayed among you as crucified?

Paul's presentation of the crucifixion was not based on what he saw with his physical eyes, but rather on the revelation he received from the Holy Spirit. His teaching was anointed, enabling those who heard him to gain a deeper understanding of the crucifixion. This understanding would not have been possible if they had witnessed it with their physical eyes. However, Paul's words were harsh because his readers had been given the message of grace, but they allowed themselves to be deceived by a works-based religion. This is a trap that many people have fallen into in their Christian journey. I have had moments when the Spirit had to correct me. However, I have always found the Spirit patient when correcting me. I encourage you to seek the Spirit's guidance to help you pursue the pure message of the cross and know He will help you just as He has me.

Chapter 9

It Is Always about Jesus and Not You

You crazy Galatians! Did someone put a spell on you? Have you taken leave of your senses? Something crazy has happened, for it's obvious that you no longer have the crucified Jesus in clear focus in your lives. His sacrifice on the cross was certainly set before you clearly enough.

GALATIANS 3:1 (THE MESSAGE)

In today's world, numerous distractions are competing for our attention. From TV shows to dozens of news channels, work responsibilities, social media, and more, it becomes difficult for Christians to focus on their relationship with God. People are so engrossed in their daily tasks that they hardly find time to read the Word of God and spend time with Him.

The Message translation of Galatians 3:1 suggests that the Galatian believers lost focus on the crucified Jesus, which led to their situation. Similarly, believers today often find themselves in such a situation. Many only call on Jesus when in a crisis and rarely think of Him outside of church when things are going well. How many people do we know who clearly understand Christ's completed redemptive work on the cross? Unfortunately, based on my experience, the number is far lower than it should be.

Our Focus Should Be on the Cross Alone

Christians often tend to focus more on what they need to do for Jesus to receive His blessing and favor rather than what Jesus did for them. Unfortunately, this mindset is not confined to just those sitting in the pews. Ministers are equally guilty of preaching a works-based Christianity, often because they are living this way in their personal lives. It is essential to be vigilant and avoid falling into this trap.

When I was younger, I struggled with a terrible sense of self-worth. I found it difficult to believe that God would accept me or even use me. As a result, my relationship with God was based on the barter system. I would plead with Him to have mercy on me and give me a drop of His anointing. In return, I promised to fast, pray at least an hour a day, and perform all sorts of rituals. Unfortunately, these efforts did nothing to ease the condemnation that I felt.

I was attempting to earn God's favor and blessing because I did not have a revelation of the cross. In my experience, most Christians are doing the same thing because they are lacking clear teaching about the cross of Christ. Our entire relationship with God should be focused on the cross and what Christ's death, burial, and resurrection has provided for us. If we focus on Jesus and all He has done for us, then we would find people living much holier lives, serving God out of love, not obligation.

So-called "soul-winning" and ministry today often focuses on what God will not do for us rather than what He has already done for us. Unfortunately, I have heard Christians say that God would withhold His love and anointing from those who have sinned or made even the slightest mistake. We should not be using fear to drive people toward God, and it should not surprise us that so many are struggling in their Christian journey as a result.

God Accepts Us Because of the Cross

Can you imagine the difference it would make if we focused on the goodness of God rather than our inability to please Him? John 3:16 tells us that God's love for humanity drove Him to send Jesus to the cross, making it possible for us to be restored into a relationship with our loving heavenly Father. Our works and religious disciplines cannot make God love us more. Paul also tells us that through Jesus, we have been made "accepted," (Ephesians 1:6) which means that God will never reject us, even when we mess up.

It's important to remember that we cannot earn a greater level of love from God. The Holy Spirit has sealed us into Christ, and as a result, God only sees us through the completed work of the cross, not through our efforts to please Him. He anointed Jesus, and through our position in Him, we have the ability to walk in Jesus' anointing.

However, we must be cautious. We have free will, and we can choose to step out of our position in Christ and harden our hearts against God. We cannot begin to imagine how much it must hurt God when someone rejects Him and chooses to move away from His presence.

It's important to remember that grace does not give us the right to live any way we want. While God's love for us will never change, sin can harden our hearts and make it difficult to fellowship with Him. Living holy lives that are separated to God is necessary.

Ultimately, a revelation of the cross will transform our approach to God. We will find ourselves living holier lives, loving God more, and serving Him without even thinking about it.

The Issue of Circumcision

Paul communicates a powerful message through the book of Galatians that repeatedly emphasizes the futility of self-righteous actions.

His aim was to help his readers understand the message of the cross clearly. For example, in Galatians 5:11, he reiterates this message once more:

> And I, brethren, if I still preach circumcision, why do I still suffer persecution? Then the offense of the cross has ceased.

Circumcision was a controversial topic for the early Christian church. The practice was first mentioned in Genesis 17, where God instructed all male descendants of Abraham to be circumcised as a sign of their covenant. Jewish leaders were strict in enforcing this practice, and it was unthinkable for someone to not get circumcised after accepting Christ if they had not been circumcised previously. The Jewish people believed that a man could not have a relationship with God if they were uncircumcised, and the early Christians adopted this belief. However, this all changed after a conference was held in Jerusalem, which is recorded in Acts 15:

> Now the apostles and elders came together to consider this matter. And when there had been much dispute, Peter rose up *and* said to them: "Men *and* brethren, you know that a good while ago God chose among us, that by my mouth the Gentiles should hear the word of the gospel and believe. So God, who knows the heart, acknowledged them by giving them the Holy Spirit, just as *He did* to us, and made no distinction between us and them, purifying their hearts by faith. Now therefore, why do you test God by putting a yoke on the neck of the disciples which neither our fathers nor we were able to bear? But we believe that through the grace of the Lord Jesus Christ we shall be saved in the same manner as they." (Acts 15:6–11)

This meeting was initiated by a group of Pharisees who had become believers and were demanding that all new believers undergo circumcision (Acts 15:5). They were concerned about the increasing number of Gentile believers who were turning to Christ in Paul's meetings but were uncircumcised. Peter, Paul, and Barnabas were in favor of grace, while the Pharisees were in favor of a works-based religion. The arguments put forth by Peter and Paul were so effective that the entire church decided to end the requirement of circumcision as a means of establishing a relationship with God.

I understand that circumcision may seem like an unusual topic to bring up today. However, it is still an important issue, as the argument made by the Pharisees regarding circumcision is still prevalent today. Nowadays, the argument has shifted to practices such as water baptism, fasting, or praying for an hour every day. It almost feels as if we are trying to reach the same destination as the Pharisees in Acts 15 but using different means of transportation.

Chapter 10

Persecution and the True Gospel

And I, brethren, if I still preach circumcision, why do I still suffer persecution? Then the offense of the cross has ceased. I could wish that those who trouble you would even cut themselves off!

GALATIANS 5:11–12

I have read numerous commentaries on Galatians 5:11–12, but none of them seem to be courageous enough to acknowledge what Paul is speaking about. Being a Jewish scholar, Paul would have been aware of Exodus 31:14, which instructed Israel to cut off any person who did not observe the Sabbath. The verse in Exodus goes so far as to command that anyone found guilty of not observing the Sabbath be put to death. Based on this, we can understand that Paul might be referring to killing those who may cause trouble to his readers and divert their attention from the cross. I understand this may sound harsh, but it aligns with the Old Testament thinking. We can consider another example in 2 Kings 19:35:

> And it came to pass on a certain night that the angel of the LORD went out, and killed in the camp of the Assyrians one hundred and eighty-five thousand; and when *people* arose early in the morning, there were the corpses—all dead.

Paul did not actually mean that he wanted those people to harm themselves or be put to death. Rather, he was trying to emphasize how grave the situation was for those who were causing trouble for the Galatian believers, as they were diverting their focus from Christ to self-righteous deeds.

The True Gospel Will
Attract Persecution

In Galatians 5, Paul referred to a performance-based gospel. He stated that anyone who teaches a message that requires living a certain way in order to be accepted or used by God has fallen into the same trap. Unfortunately, this message is still prevalent today. Those who preach the true message of grace will be persecuted by those who adhere to the performance-based gospel. This was true in Paul's time, and it remains true today.

If you have a revelation of the cross and begin to teach the true gospel, you can expect to be persecuted. Religious individuals who are held back by these spirits will be first in line to do so, just as they were in the days of Jesus and the early church.

Modern Christian messaging has shifted toward an easy gospel that is nonconfrontational. This is a widely accepted norm that receives little pushback from the world. It is only those who preach the true gospel who are being persecuted. However, this should not come as a surprise. Jesus was hounded by the Pharisees and Sadducees for the message He taught, and the early Christians were also treated terribly for preaching the gospel message. Therefore, we should not expect it to be any different for us today.

God Desires Only
Good for His Children

I once heard Oral Roberts say that the thing that caused the most opposition to the message he preached was his insistence to start his television broadcast with the statement, "God's got something good for you today." It has always amazed me how much it upsets people when anyone preaches the goodness of God. The truth is, God sent Jesus to the cross to pay the complete price for our sins. Hebrews 9:11 tells us that Jesus came as God's "High Priest of the good things to come." *Agathos* is the Greek word translated as "good" in this verse, describing anything that is good in nature and originates from God through faith, which is always received as a gift from Him.

The message of the cross declares God's goodness toward humanity. Jesus paid the entire price, so our attempts to turn the focus toward human works pollute the gospel message. Religious teaching often emphasizes performance, but the idea that we can freely receive God's blessings through the measure of faith He has given us (Romans 12:3) can be extremely offensive to those who have worn themselves out trying to serve Him. People who have tried to earn God's favor may struggle to accept the message of grace because it requires them to admit that their hard work has done nothing to increase God's willingness to accept them.

Ephesians 1:6 states that Jesus has made us acceptable to the Father through grace. This means that God accepts everyone in the same way, regardless of their past or present circumstances. Jesus completed the work of salvation through His death, burial, and resurrection, which opened the door for us to find rest in Him. However, many people still struggle to receive from God because they approach Him with a mindset of lists and formulas focused on their own goodness rather than on the merit of Christ's completed work.

Some people who are trying to get a healing from God do not understand that He has already provided it, and so they stand and wait for Him to move. They may wear themselves out following checklists and formulas, but they will never experience God's healing power. In contrast, people who come to God without any preconceived notions, such as the homeless or alcoholics, often experience miraculous healing and deliverance instantly. These people usually have not been inundated with religious tradition and therefore do not struggle with believing God like those who have been.

Living a holy life is beneficial, but it will not cause God to favor you over others. Those who have a revelation of the cross tend to live much holier lives out of a sense of love for God and appreciation for what He has provided for them in Jesus' redemptive work.

Christ Died to Set Us Free from Religious Works

Galatians 5:11–12 addresses circumcision, which is no longer a relevant issue today. However, Paul's argument is still applicable to other religious traditions. The issue has changed, but the argument remains the same. Christians still tend to pursue a works-based mentality, which Jesus died on the cross to set us free from. This mentality is rooted in a law-based approach that focuses on our actions, instead of the work Jesus accomplished on the cross.

We have already received the anointing, favor, and blessing of God in Christ, even before we accepted Him as our Lord and Savior. There's nothing we can do to change this. Some people enjoy greater levels of blessing simply because they have taken the time to renew their minds to what has already been provided in Christ Jesus. You, too, can walk in the fullness of what has been provided for you on the cross. The only requirement is turning our focus away from our own works and toward the cross. Everything in our Christian journey should be about what Jesus has already done for us rather than what we can do for Him.

People who are steeped in self-righteousness tend to focus on themselves and what they are doing for God. They find it offensive to think they can do nothing to earn more anointing, favor, or pull with God through their efforts. They have based their entire Christian theology on the belief that it's possible to gain more leverage with God by doing more for Him. These people struggle to accept the fact that our standing is based on Christ's work on the cross alone.

It takes humility to accept that all our goodness is nothing compared to Jesus'. The self-righteous mentality will never agree to lay down its success, goodness, and pride at the feet of the cross. You will never know true freedom, though, until you lay everything before Him and admit that you are no better than the drug addict, homosexual, or homeless alcoholic. Paul refers to this act as the time when we become "a living sacrifice" in Romans 12:1. It's the point where we lose ourselves in Him and He can pour His glory through us to the lost and dying world around us.

Standing in the Liberty by Which Christ Has Made Us Free

I have had the pleasure of meeting many wonderful people in various churches over the years who love God and desire to serve Him. Many of them follow spiritual practices and read Bible plans that are provided by their churches. However, I have also noticed that a significant number of Christians I've met tend to live their lives outside of the church in a way that is similar to their non-Christian neighbors. After observing this pattern over time, I have come to realize that this is largely because they have not humbled themselves to become completely dependent on Jesus and what He has done for them.

Many people fail to humble themselves because they lack an understanding of the message of the cross. Paul's words in Galatians 5:1 illustrate this point:

> Stand fast therefore in the liberty by which Christ has made us free, and do not be entangled again with a yoke of bondage.

The message of the cross is truly liberating, as it frees people from the bondages they have suffered under. This freedom enables us to live in a way that many people seek today but do not find. In my early years, I was reluctant to accept the message of grace due to the many instances of its abuse by ministers. However, with the help of the Holy Spirit, I have come to appreciate the grace message. One of the criticisms against preachers of grace is that they encourage people to live in sin. While it is true that some ministers have done this, it is also true that those who truly understand grace will live a holier life, not out of obligation, but out of their love for God and appreciation for all He has provided them in Christ Jesus.

I don't believe preaching about grace in the context of the cross will cause people to live in sin. This is discussed by Paul in Titus 2:11–12:

> For the grace of God that brings salvation has appeared to all men, *teaching us that, denying ungodliness and worldly lusts, we should live soberly, righteously, and godly in the present age.* (Emphasis added)

A true understanding of grace in your heart will lead you to live a life that is characterized by sobriety, righteousness, and godliness. This is contrary to what critics of the grace message argue. However, one of the major issues in the church today is that only a few ministers who teach grace have gained a true revelation of this knowledge. Specifically, they haven't grasped the revelation that Christ died to set us free from the yoke of bondage and open the door to an intimate relationship with our creator. This relationship is based solely on the work of Jesus on the cross.

Chapter 11

Has the Church Strayed from the Message of the Cross?

*Brethren, join in following my example, and note
those who so walk, as you have us for a pattern.*

PHILIPPIANS 3:17

The apostle Paul was so confident in his message and his relationship with God that he encouraged his readers to follow his example. In Philippians 3:17, Paul boldly suggests that his followers use him as a model for following Christ. Nowadays, such a statement might be seen as arrogant, but Paul's confidence stemmed from an understanding that his identity was in Christ rather than in his own accomplishments and achievements. This realization allowed him to make such confident statements.

One Gospel Message

I marvel that you are turning away so soon from Him who called you in the grace of Christ, to a different gospel, which is not another; but there are some who trouble you and want to pervert the gospel of Christ. But even if we, or an angel from heaven, preach any other gospel to you than what we have preached to you, let him be accursed. As we have said before, so now I say again, if anyone preaches any other gospel to you than what you have received, let him be accursed. (Galatians 1:6–9)

Paul was very sure of himself when he delivered his message to the believers in Galatia. He even went so far to say that anyone who preached a different message would be "accursed." This is powerful language. Paul was certain of what he was preaching, and we can learn a valuable lesson from his conviction. I believe that anyone who is not as sure about their understanding of Christ as Paul was should not be preaching. There is only one gospel message, and it revolves around the cross.

There are many ministers today who simply repeat what they have learned or read in a commentary without spending enough time communing with the Holy Spirit. Most of them have lost the ability to preach from a position of revelation. I can't help but wonder what Paul would think of the current state of affairs. We have even gotten to the point where many denominations offer pre-written sermons for their ministers to spare them from having to prepare their own.

Enemies of the Cross

I believe that most Christians desire to see the power of God working in greater measures. However, do you believe that this can happen if we are not preaching the same message that Paul preached? According to Mark 16:20, the Lord worked with the disciples and confirmed the Word "through the accompanying signs." He did not confirm their theology or religious practices. Therefore, we should pay attention to Paul's words in Philippians 3:18–19:

For many walk, of whom I have told you often, and now tell you even weeping, *that they are the enemies of the cross of Christ*: whose end is destruction, whose god is *their* belly, and *whose* glory *is* in their shame—who set their mind on earthly things. (Emphasis added in v. 18)

This is a strongly worded statement, isn't it? Some individuals tend to create controversy by preaching certain topics. However, Paul was not one of those people. The way this statement is phrased indicates that he didn't enjoy having to write it any more than you or I would. We can find other similar examples of such statements in Paul's writings. One such instance is in Romans 10:2–3:

> For I bear them witness that they have a zeal for God, but not according to knowledge. For they being ignorant of God's righteousness, and seeking to establish their own righteousness, have not submitted to the righteousness of God.

He was referring to the Jewish people who were enthusiastic in their desire to serve God but unaware of the revelation that their Messiah had already arrived. Paul could sympathize with these people because he had been one of them before he turned to Christ.

In this passage, Paul expresses that he was heartbroken to the point of tears to label certain individuals as "the enemies of the cross of Christ" (Philippians 3:18). He recognized the gravity of their situation, as indicated in verse 19, where he described their end as "destruction." Paul was referring to religious people who boasted about their own achievements and holiness and looked down upon others. They derived their pride from their fleshly accomplishments rather than placing their faith in Christ.

Developing an Eternal Perspective

I believe that people often overemphasize their accomplishments because they lack eternal perspective. Our perspective would change if we viewed our time on Earth as just a moment in eternity. Psalm 78:39 (KJV) offers a glimpse of humanity from God's perspective. If you ever experience His perspective, you will realize that all your achievements no longer matter.

> For he remembered that they were but flesh; a wind that passeth away, and cometh not again.

God understands that we are human and have a fleshly nature. However, over the years, I have met many people who live with self-inflicted condemnation. They do not comprehend the message of the cross and believe that God could never accept them based on their performance. It is our responsibility to share the good news that Jesus has paid the complete price for our salvation, freeing us from works-based religion. He has opened the door to moving away from religious works toward a personal relationship with Him, and He is only waiting for us to take that step.

The Spiritual and Carnal Mindsets

> In the year that king Uzziah died I saw also the LORD sitting upon a throne, high and lifted up, and his train filled the temple. Above it stood the seraphims: each one had six wings; with twain he covered his face, and with twain he covered his feet, and with twain he did fly. And one cried unto another, and said, Holy, holy, holy, is the LORD of hosts: the whole earth is full of his glory. And the posts of the door moved at the voice of him that cried, and the house was filled with smoke. Then said I, Woe is me! for I am undone; because I am a man of unclean lips, and I dwell in the midst of a people of unclean lips: for mine eyes have seen the King, the LORD of hosts. (Isaiah 6:1–5 KJV)

Notice Isaiah's reaction when he saw the glory of God. I believe it is a natural response for any human being who has been confronted with God's glory. Immediately, we will recognize how unworthy we are to stand in God's presence. People who boast about their accomplishments and the things they have done for God have no sense of His glory. I believe they are the people Paul referred to in Philippians 3:19:

> Whose glory *is* in their shame—who set their mind on earthly things.

You will find that people who promote the need to live holy lives for God in order for Him to love or use us in His service are glorying in their shame. They have their minds set on earthly things and do not understand the message of the cross. Paul refers to this mindset as "carnal" in Romans 8:5–8:

> For those who live according to the flesh set their minds on the things of the flesh, but those who live according to the Spirit, the things of the Spirit. For to be carnally minded is death, but to be spiritually minded is life and peace. Because the carnal mind is enmity against God; for it is not subject to the law of God, nor indeed can be. So then, those who are in the flesh cannot please God.

It is impossible to continuously focus on the natural realm and consistently experience the power of God. Many people have tried this but failed. I believe this is the reason why Paul tells us that it is impossible to walk in the flesh and please God. Those who are carnally minded tend to focus their attention on natural matters and rarely think of spiritual things unless in service or when facing a crisis.

Who Are the Enemies of the Cross?

We discussed Philippians 3:18–19 and talked briefly about those who have become enemies of the cross, but now I want to revisit this phrase with a focus on determining who exactly the enemies of the cross are. While people of other faiths, such Islam or Hindu, could be considered enemies of the cross, what about Christians? Is it possible for a believer to turn against the cross of Christ?

In his letter to the Philippians, Paul addressed the issue of Jews who had converted to Christianity but still believed in the need to keep the Old Testament Law to gain God's favor. These individuals did not believe that Jesus' death was enough to save them from their sins. Paul referred to them as enemies of the cross. If someone accused me of being an enemy of the cross, I would feel uncertain about how to respond.

The Jewish converts were not intentionally misleading people away from the message of the cross. They were operating with the level of revelation that they had and probably believed that what they were teaching was correct. Many Christians today have also fallen into the same trap of adding to the gospel message without realizing it. Although they have good intentions, they need to be corrected, just like Paul corrected the Jewish believers of his day. We are all on a journey together and should never condemn or criticize anyone. Instead, our goal should always be to lead people to the Holy Spirit and allow Him to help them get on track.

If we were to accuse some churchgoers of being an enemy of the cross of Christ, they would be highly offended. Wouldn't you? The sad truth is that the majority of Christians do not realize they have adopted religious traditions that are contrary to the cross. This includes anyone who places the burden of salvation on people instead of the cross. They do this by requiring religious activities such as taking the sacrament or reciting liturgies. For instance, the Catholic Church practices the sacrament of Confession, which is believed to cleanse a person of their sins and renew their position in Christ. In other words, some people believe that the blood of Jesus is insufficient to cleanse them of their sins. Therefore, they must also partake in this practice to receive total reconciliation.

Chapter 12

The Dangers of Self-Righteousness

Finally, my brethren, rejoice in the Lord. For me to write the
same things to you is *not tedious, but for you* it is *safe.*

PHILIPPIANS 3:1

Propaganda can often be spread by repeatedly stating lies until they are perceived as truth. Similarly, religious traditions can also become ingrained in people's minds through repetition. When individuals attend church and hear such traditions taught from the pulpit every week, they may eventually believe that what they hear is biblically sound. To protect ourselves, we must consistently refer to Scripture as we listen to our ministers, and use what we find to evaluate what we are being exposed to about God's Word.

In the previous chapters, we established that our relationship with God is solely based on what Jesus did for us. Our religious works do not affect His love for us in any way. The only reason He accepts us is because of the blood of Christ that was shed on the cross. These truths bear repeating because they are entirely different from what most churches teach nowadays.

In Philippians 3:2, Paul continues his train of thought with a statement I initially found difficult to understand:

Beware of dogs, beware of evil workers, beware of the mutilation!

In the King James Version of the Bible, the term *mutilation* is used interchangeably with *circumcision*. Although I am not an expert in biblical language, Paul's statement is of great importance. He was highly critical in his assessment of these individuals. As we have seen in the previous chapter, Paul referred to them as the enemies of the cross. Their teachings and religious practices were completely contradictory to the work of Christ on the cross. They had replaced the true gospel message with religious tradition, as so many have done today.

Intercession and Religious Traditions

An example of a typical religious tradition being taught today is our approach to intercession. The focus of most teaching on this subject centers on Old Testament accounts of intercession. Exodus 32:7–14 is one passage commonly referenced by these teachers:

And the LORD said to Moses, "Go, get down! For your people whom you brought out of the land of Egypt have corrupted *themselves*. They have turned aside quickly out of the way which I commanded them. They have made themselves a molded calf, and worshiped it and sacrificed to it, and said, 'This *is* your god, O Israel, that brought you out of the land of Egypt!'" And the LORD said to Moses, "I have seen this people, and indeed it *is* a stiff-necked people! Now therefore, let Me alone, that My wrath may burn hot against them and I may consume them. And I will make of you a great nation." Then Moses pleaded with the LORD his God, and said: "LORD, why does Your wrath burn hot against Your people whom You have brought out of the land of Egypt with great power and with a mighty hand? Why should the Egyptians speak, and say, 'He brought them out to harm them, to kill them in the mountains, and to consume them from the face of the earth'? Turn from Your fierce wrath, and relent from this harm to Your people. Remember Abraham, Isaac, and Israel, Your servants, to whom You swore by Your own self, and said to them, 'I will multiply your descendants as the stars of heaven; and all this land that I have spoken of I give to your descendants, and they shall inherit *it* forever.'" So the LORD relented from the harm which He said He would do to His people.

How can we reconcile the example of Moses seen in these verses with teachings that seem to contradict the message of the cross? Some people use Moses' example to argue that we need to intercede on behalf of our country, family, and nonbelievers to protect them from God's wrath, just as he stood in the gap for Israel. They often cite Galatians 3:19–20 to support their position:

What purpose then *does* the law *serve*? It was added because of transgressions, till the Seed should come to whom the promise was made; *and it was* appointed through angels by the hand of a mediator. Now a mediator does not *mediate* for one *only*, but God is one.

Moses acted as a mediator between God and Israel before Jesus arrived and paid for our sins on the cross. A mediator's role is to reconcile two opposing sides, and Moses stood in to appease the wrath of God, thus saving the nation of Israel. However, since Moses lived before the cross, it was suitable for him to pray as he did. Today, we live after the cross, and as mentioned in 1 Timothy 2:5, there is only "one Mediator between God and men, *the* Man Christ Jesus." Those who teach the necessity to stand in the gap today ignore this verse. In the new covenant, the only mediator between God and man is Jesus.

Are We Willing to Stand for the Message of the Cross?

Jesus acted as a mediator between humanity and God by sacrificing Himself, being buried, and resurrected from the dead. He pleaded our case before God, paid the price for our sins, and reconciled us with God. Therefore, we don't need to plead with God or act as mediators because Jesus has already done that for us. Those who teach intercessory prayer from the perspective of Old Testament saints like Moses or Abraham are going against the work of the cross. They are encouraging people to take on a role that Jesus has already fulfilled. This approach to intercession is equivalent to resisting the work of Christ on the cross and unknowingly yielding to the spirit of antichrist.

I understand that my beliefs about intercession may not align with commonly taught practices, and may even offend some people. Some may argue that the intentions behind intercessory practices are good, and we should be lenient toward those who follow them, as they are at least engaging in prayer instead of idle activities. However, in the past, people may have argued similarly regarding Paul's letter to the Galatian Christians. I acknowledge that there is a place for intercession in the new covenant, but I am against the way modern intercessors often teach the subject.

Paul was a bold truth speaker who didn't hesitate to call out people who taught a different message than that of the cross. He even referred to them as "dogs" and "evil workers" in some of his letters (Philippians 3:2). In today's culture, we tend to prioritize making people comfortable in church, but we can learn from Paul's approach.

We have compromised the message of the cross and lost our willingness to stand boldly for the truth of Scripture. It's time for us to stop giving people a pass for their good intentions and start preaching the truth of the Bible, just as Paul and the early church did.

Paul's letters often contained strong language, and he wasn't afraid to call people out when necessary. One of the recurring themes in his writing is the importance of putting our faith in Christ alone. In this context, we will examine Philippians 3:3–6:

> For we are the circumcision, who worship God in the Spirit, rejoice in Christ Jesus, and have no confidence in the flesh, though I also might have confidence in the flesh. If anyone else thinks he may have confidence in the flesh, I more so: circumcised the eighth day, of the stock of Israel, *of* the tribe of Benjamin, a Hebrew of the Hebrews; concerning the law, a Pharisee; concerning zeal, persecuting the church; concerning the righteousness which is in the law, blameless.

Some people believe that religious rituals are necessary to gain God's favor. However, this belief can unwittingly create a barrier between us and God. In Philippians 3, Paul is admonishing religious Jews who believed that circumcision was necessary for salvation. Even today, some preach that we must live a holy life or keep certain sacraments to maintain God's favor and avoid His wrath. However, they have missed the true meaning of the cross and the gospel taught by the church fathers such as Paul and Peter. We cannot judge these misguided preachers, as we are all equally susceptible to the temptation of doing the same thing.

An Example of Righteousness

The book of Hebrews teaches that God uses correction to develop righteousness in us:

Now no chastening seems to be joyful for the present, but painful; nevertheless, afterward it yields the peaceable fruit of righteousness to those who have been trained by it. Therefore strengthen the hands which hang down, and the feeble knees, and make straight paths for your feet, so that what is lame may not be dislocated, but rather be healed. Pursue peace with all *people*, and holiness, without which no one will see the Lord: looking carefully lest anyone fall short of the grace of God; lest any root of bitterness springing up cause trouble, and by this many become defiled; lest there be any fornicator, or profane person like Esau, who for one morsel of food sold his birthright. (Hebrews 12:11–16)

It's crucial to remember that we may come across people going through a difficult time who will require some guidance. Avoiding being judgmental or overly critical of them is essential. Instead, our aim should be to motivate and inspire them while still holding onto our belief in the truth. Paul's letters are an excellent example of this. Even though his words could be forceful at times, his overall message was always focused on encouraging the reader. We should learn from his example.

The writer of Hebrews emphasizes the significance of setting an excellent example in the verses that come before and after Hebrews 12:14. It is crucial to live our lives in a manner that inspires and encourages those around us. We should strive to reflect God's character in us, and I believe this is what the writer means in verse 14:

Pursue peace with all *people*, and holiness, without which no one will see the Lord:

I have heard ministers quote a verse from the Bible to emphasize the importance of living a holy life. However, they often claim that no one can see heaven without first living a holy life. This claim does not consider the context of Hebrews 12:14. The writer of Hebrews is telling us that our holiness should be a testimony that leads others to the Lord. People should see God working in our lives and be encouraged that He will bless them just as He has blessed us.

Unfortunately, the message of the cross in today's religious systems has been twisted. We have added requirements such as living holy or adhering to spiritual disciplines dictated by our religious leadership, which goes against the redemptive work of Jesus. Paul addressed this issue in Philippians 3:17–21 when he spoke of those who became "enemies of the cross." Our focus should always be on what Jesus has done for us, not on what we can do for Him.

It's worth noting that Paul was speaking to Gentile converts in the book of Philippians. In verse 3, he makes an interesting statement: "We are the circumcision." This statement might have been offensive to religious Jews who claimed to be the true people of God. After all, God's covenant was with Abraham, not the forefathers of the Gentiles.

There seems to be a connection between Philippians 3:17–21 and Paul's statement in Romans 2:25:

> For circumcision is indeed profitable if you keep the law; but if you are a breaker of the law, your circumcision has become uncircumcision.

Paul's message to his readers was quite simple and straightforward. Our good deeds and acts of holiness won't earn us any additional favor from God. God's opinion of us is based solely on the sacrifice of Christ on the cross. Therefore, when we try to win His love through our actions, it implies that we don't believe Christ was sufficient. That's why Paul tells us that our good deeds become unholy. They are unspoken statements that God did not fully redeem us through Jesus' death, burial, and resurrection.

It often feels like our lives are being judged on a balance of fairness. On one side are our good deeds, and on the other, our bad ones. Many Christians believe in this and are always striving to gain God's favor. They feel that their bad deeds always outweigh the good ones, making the balance lean toward negativity. I used to think this way for many years, and I understand very well how it can prevent a person from experiencing the peace that comes from resting in Christ's finished work.

Complete Dependence on Christ

James teaches that even if someone fails in one small area of the Law, they will be judged guilty of the entire Law (James 2:10). This means that no one can meet the standard set by the Law, which is why the cross was necessary. Under the old covenant, a person's works would be considered unholy if they missed it in any area, and as a result, no one could approach God based on their own goodness. Today, we can only access God through the blood of Christ because our goodness cannot give us access to Him now any more than it could back then.

Some ministers strongly believe that to be born again, we must completely trust Jesus. I agree with them on this point. However, the issue arises when many of these men and women insist that we are responsible for maintaining our salvation through our holiness. This viewpoint is incorrect, as we have seen several verses in the Bible prove. Paul provides us with further insight into this matter in Colossians 2:6:

> As you therefore have received Christ Jesus the Lord, so walk in Him.

The verse stresses the significance of maintaining a constant relationship with God even after we have been saved. Our salvation depends on our complete faith in Jesus, and we must continue to depend on Him throughout our lives. To receive salvation, we must acknowledge our own helplessness without Jesus. However, when we forget our dependence on Him after salvation, Satan can hinder our experience of God's fullness in our lives. This is the position many people find themselves in when they rely on their own good works to gain God's favor. It is also the reason why many individuals live under a constant cloud of condemnation.

If you feel condemned, it may be because you are not relying on your position in Christ Jesus. Instead, you might have shifted from grace to self-righteousness. This shift leads to a performance-based relationship where you rely entirely on yourself. In Romans 2:25, Paul tries to explain that circumcision represents our self-righteous works. He told his audience that their self-righteous works would only be helpful if they could live without missing even one small part of the Law, which we know is impossible.

Chapter 13

What Is the Condition of Your Heart?

*For circumcision is indeed profitable if you keep the law; but if you
are a breaker of the law, your circumcision has become uncircumcision.
Therefore, if an uncircumcised man keeps the righteous requirements
of the law, will not his uncircumcision be counted as circumcision?
And will not the physically uncircumcised, if he fulfills the law, judge
you who,* even *with* your *written* code *and circumcision,* are *a
transgressor of the law? For he is not a Jew who* is one *outwardly, nor*
is *circumcision that which* is *outward in the flesh; but* he is *a Jew
who* is one *inwardly; and circumcision* is that *of the heart, in the
Spirit, not in the letter; whose praise* is *not from men but from God.*

ROMANS 2:25–29

On the surface, this passage seems quite confusing, doesn't it? In
plain English: There are people we may consider to be unholy
who have a closer relationship with God than those who live moral
lives and seem to be the most holy among us. I think about a man
named Paul who was saved in a meeting I held. He came from a very
rough background and did not fit the mold of what most Christians
would consider to be holy. One night a lady came to the altar to have
the pastor and I pray for a huge tumor on her neck. Paul approached
the pastor and asked if he could pray for her. He agreed, and, to our
horror, he ran toward the lady shouting some very profane things at

the tumor on her neck. We were absolutely shocked to see the tumor fly off her as soon as Paul touched her. She was instantly healed, but the vessel through which the healing power flowed was not what we would have considered to be one clean enough for God to use.

During a church service, Paul said some things that were not considered appropriate. However, an incredible miracle occurred. Unfortunately, some people later complained to the pastor about Paul's approach, judging him based on their perception of his holiness. Fortunately, God judged Paul based on his heart, not external holiness. I can imagine the Lord sitting on His throne, laughing at our self-righteous attitude toward how Paul ministered to the woman. After the service, the Holy Spirit told me that He was more pleased with Paul than any other person who had prayed for the sick. In other words, the profanity used to address the tumor was more effective than all the other religious terminology used in our prayers in the Lord's eyes.

Circumcision of the Heart

In Romans 2:29, we learn that the true Jew is one who has undergone circumcision of the heart. This statement must have been highly offensive to the Jewish people of Paul's time since they based their judgments on external actions. They deemed a person's worth based on factors such as their Jewish lineage and their observance of feast days. However, Paul prioritized the condition of the heart over such external factors.

The true Jew today is someone who has received Jesus and has been circumcised in their heart. However, it is crucial to be careful in presenting this truth. Some people have taken it to an extreme and claimed that the church has replaced Israel. This view is often referred to as replacement theology, which is not supported by Paul in his letters. There are still promises for Israel backed by the covenant, but the Bible refers to the church today as the people of God. We did not replace the Jewish people; instead, we were grafted into the new covenant that God had established for them, which was sealed with the blood of Jesus on the cross.

Paul emphasizes in Galatians 2:1–5 that he received the gospel message by revelation of the Spirit:

> Then after fourteen years I went up again to Jerusalem with Barnabas, and also took Titus with *me*. And I went up by revelation and communicated to them that gospel which I preach among the Gentiles, but privately to those who were of reputation, lest by any means I might run, or had run, in vain. Yet not even Titus who *was* with me, being a Greek, was compelled to be circumcised. And *this occurred* because of false brethren secretly brought in (who came in by stealth to spy out our liberty which we have in Christ Jesus, that they might bring us into bondage), to whom we did not yield submission even for an hour, that the truth of the gospel might continue with you.

In Acts 15, we learn that Paul traveled to Jerusalem to attend a council meeting. At this meeting, some attendees were spreading the false idea that one cannot be saved without being circumcised according to the custom of Moses. Paul's purpose for attending this meeting was to counter this false teaching. The people who were spreading this teaching were Jewish believers who did not understand the message of the cross. They preached a works-based approach to the cross, which was influenced by their religious backgrounds. Since circumcision was mandatory for Jewish males, they could not accept the idea of a Christian male not being circumcised.

Religious Pharisees

There are individuals in the church who judge others based on what they can see with their physical eyes, missing the grace of God that works in the heart. Religious Pharisees are still present in the church, teaching religious tradition behind the pulpit week after week, although their titles may have changed. In Philippians 3, Paul talks about people who impose religious works as a prerequisite on those who have already accepted Jesus as their Lord. In Paul's time, the primary topic of debate was circumcision. However, nowadays we encounter people who argue that God only accepts the King James translation of the Bible, that women cannot be preachers, or that other external requirements must be met to gain God's favor. These proponents are missing the central message of grace. There will always be individuals in the church who are so entrenched in their religious traditions that they cannot accept the gospel message. They are the ones who criticize and nitpick every little thing they see happening in service each week, complaining about hairstyles, makeup, or jewelry. Paul refers to them as "evil workers" in Philippians 3:2 and advises us to avoid them. He lived a holy life even before his conversion to Christianity, and he makes this argument in Philippians 3:2–6:

> Beware of dogs, beware of evil workers, beware of the mutilation! For we are the circumcision, who worship God in the Spirit, rejoice in Christ Jesus, and have no confidence in the flesh, though I also might have confidence in the flesh. If anyone else thinks he may have confidence in the flesh, I more so: circumcised the eighth day, of the stock of Israel, of the tribe of Benjamin, a Hebrew of the Hebrews; concerning the law, a Pharisee; concerning zeal, persecuting the church; concerning the righteousness which is in the law, blameless.

Paul argued that he was a moral and good man according to the Law before meeting Jesus on the Damascus Road (Acts 9). His statements show that he obeyed the Law and followed every religious tradition taught by the Jewish leaders. This resulted in his rise in the ranks of the Pharisees, but it did not earn him salvation or the forgiveness of sins. In Philippians 3:7, Paul reveals that he had realized that all his success and good work meant nothing compared to the cross of Christ. Therefore, he considered it all as a "loss for Christ." Can any of us say the same things about our natural accomplishments and how we view them?

The phrase *I have counted loss for Christ* mentioned in Philippians 3:7 is quite intriguing. Paul used a term from the business world—*loss*—that is typically used to describe an unsuccessful transaction that incurs a penalty. Today, many people take pride in their accomplishments and good works done in the name of Christ. They may not realize it, but they have adopted the mindset of the religious Pharisees from Paul's time. I have heard such people boast about things like the hours they spend in prayer or how many times they have read through the Bible. However, Paul's statement is quite different from theirs. He had a deep understanding of the value of knowing Christ, and he was willing to sacrifice everything else to gain it.

Turning away from Self-Righteousness

In this book, I have discussed the issue of self-righteousness in our ranks. While practices like taking communion, attending church regularly, or leading a holy life are not wrong, putting our trust in these things can become burdensome. Many people believe in their own goodness and think that their religious acts make them worthy of being used by God. However, as we can see in Philippians 3:7, Paul came to the realization that all his accomplishments, education, and success were worthless in comparison to the cross of

Christ. Can we say the same thing today about our attitude toward our accomplishments?

In Philippians 3:9, Paul expresses his desire to be discovered in Jesus, not possessing his own righteousness, but instead, having "the righteousness which is from God by faith." Self-righteousness is always based on our ability to follow some sort of religious standard, but trying to measure up to someone else's standard will not grant us the freedom that is accessible to us through the cross. True freedom can only be found in Christ, and I believe that you have already started your journey toward finding that.

Chapter 14

The Price of Our Sin

And one of the Pharisees desired him that he would eat with him. And he went into the Pharisee's house, and sat down to meat. And, behold, a woman in the city, which was a sinner, when she knew that Jesus sat at meat in the Pharisee's house, brought an alabaster box of ointment, and stood at his feet behind him weeping, and began to wash his feet with tears, and did wipe them with the hairs of her head, and kissed his feet, and anointed them with the ointment. Now when the Pharisee which had bidden him saw it, he spake within himself, saying, This man, if he were a prophet, would have known who and what manner of woman this is that toucheth him: for she is a sinner. And Jesus answering said unto him, Simon, I have somewhat to say unto thee. And he saith, Master, say on. There was a certain creditor which had two debtors: the one owed five hundred pence, and the other fifty. And when they had nothing to pay, he frankly forgave them both. Tell me therefore, which of them will love him most? Simon answered and said, I suppose that he, to whom he forgave most. And he said unto him, Thou hast rightly judged. And he turned to the woman, and said unto Simon, Seest thou this woman? I entered into thine house, thou gavest me no water for my feet: but she hath washed my feet with tears, and wiped them with the hairs of her head. Thou gavest me no kiss: but this woman since the time I came in hath not ceased to kiss my feet. My head with oil thou didst not anoint: but this woman hath anointed my feet with ointment. Wherefore I say unto thee, Her sins, which are many, are forgiven; for she loved much: but to whom little is forgiven, the same loveth little. And he said unto her, Thy sins are forgiven.

LUKE 7:36–48 KJV

Jesus was invited to a dinner at a Pharisee's house. During the dinner, a woman who was known to be a sinner arrived and brought a box of ointment. She used the ointment to wash Jesus' feet and humbly wiped them with her hair, which upset the Pharisee. He was surprised that Jesus allowed this woman to even touch him. However, Jesus knew what the Pharisee was thinking and responded with a parable. He closed his response with the words, "Her sins, which *are* many, are forgiven; for she loved much" (Luke 7:47). This principle is also mentioned in 2 Peter 1:9:

> For he who lacks these things is shortsighted, even to blindness, and *has forgotten that he was cleansed from his old sins.* (Emphasis added)

We need to comprehend the full extent of God's forgiveness, as it enables us to love Him more deeply. This is what Jesus was attempting to convey in Luke 7. However, this subject is not frequently discussed in sermons. In this chapter, we will concentrate on the concept of hell and investigate what we have been rescued from.

Some people follow the teachings of grace and faith, and they don't believe in the concept of hell. They think it goes against their principles. However, I have been influenced by both faith and grace teachers. I know that the idea of hell doesn't contradict either camp's message. In fact, knowing what I have been saved from has made me more thankful for all that God has given me through His grace and has increased my desire to follow Him.

Some individuals may claim that they don't need much forgiveness because they have lived a virtuous life. However, it's important to understand that there is no such thing as different levels of hell with varying degrees of suffering for those who have lived a *good* life on Earth. Likewise, God does not offer different degrees of forgiveness. Jesus went to the cross and obtained an eternal redemption that is offered to all equally. If you don't make it to heaven, your destination will be hell, regardless of how you've lived on this earth. You may have been involved in charitable work, helped the homeless, or fed the poor, but none of that will matter if you don't have Jesus.

The Need to Understand What We Have Been Forgiven Of

In order to go to heaven, it is necessary to accept Jesus Christ as your Savior. If you choose not to do so, you will end up in hell after this life. The concept is quite simple to understand. We have all sinned and been forgiven because of the cross, regardless of how good or bad we may have lived our lives. Some people may compare their sins to others and believe that their sins are not as bad. You must never forget God has not established a hierarchy of sins. He views all equally. However, this does not mean that Jesus is not needed in one's life. There are no exceptions to this. Jesus is the only way to establish a relationship with God. All other paths lead to hell.

It's common for humans to compare themselves to others and judge their lives based on this comparison. However, this can be a dangerous trap to fall into. To avoid it, it's important to understand what we have been forgiven of. Some preachers who teach about grace avoid discussing the topic of hell, thinking it's not helpful. But I believe the opposite is true. Realizing the things we have been forgiven of aligns perfectly with the message of grace.

I know the eternal destination my life was heading toward. This makes me love God even more, and it makes me more appreciative of the grace of God to understand this. You will find it difficult to fully understand the grace and atonement Jesus gained for us on the cross without a similar understanding of what your eternal destination would be otherwise. If you do not understand how bad the transgression of humanity is that leads to a sentence of eternity in hell, you will never understand the love of God expressed at the cross. You will never fully appreciate Jesus' death, burial, and resurrection without first understanding how bad of a situation humanity was in because of sin.

To illustrate, consider a person who receives a fifty dollar fine for speeding. It probably wouldn't be hard for someone to cover this debt on the person's behalf. But what if the crime had been murder and the conviction death? A much greater commitment would be required for someone to suffer the penalty in their place, wouldn't it? Consequently, an offer to pay off someone else's speeding ticket would elicit a much different reaction compared to an offer to bear their death sentence.

The Penalty for Sin

Many people mistakenly believe that grace implies God is willing to overlook our sins. However, this is not true. Grace refers to the provision made by God, which was made possible through the sacrificial death of Jesus on the cross. As Paul explains in Romans 6:23, "The wages of sin *is* death." Our God is just and holy, and the penalty of sin needed to be paid for us to be reconciled with Him. Therefore, it is important to understand that sin carries a penalty. For God's justice to be satisfied, sin had to be judged.

An interesting observation is that the word *wages* in Romans 6:23 is plural, not singular. The punishment for sin dates back to the Garden of Eden, when God warned Adam not to eat from the tree of knowledge of good and evil. He told Adam that if he ate from it, he would surely die. This is because sin causes us to become separated from God, who is the source of our life (as mentioned in John 1:4). When Adam disobeyed God, he immediately became spiritually disconnected from Him, because of his sin.

It can be helpful to view death not as the end of our physical life, but as separation from God. According to Scripture, God breathed life into Adam, making him a living being (Genesis 2:7). Therefore,

God is the source of our life, and sin separates us from Him, which leads to a spiritual state referred to as death in the Bible. Spiritual death is the separation of our spirit from God, while physical death is the separation of our spirit and soul from our physical body.

When God warned Adam about the consequences of eating the forbidden fruit, He was referring to Adam and Eve's separation from Him. Before their disobedience, they enjoyed a state of complete unity and dependence on God in the garden. However, eating the forbidden fruit resulted in their disconnection from God. Their action was not simply eating an apple or any fruit, but it was an act of elevating themselves to the position of God by disregarding His command.

Spiritual Death versus Physical Death

Adam and Eve were disconnected from God the moment they ate the forbidden fruit, which ultimately caused their spiritual death. The physical dying process started in the garden itself, but their bodies took more than nine hundred years to completely die. Their disobedience severed their link with God, who was the source of life for their whole being.

I have observed some lights that continue to emit a faint glow even after being disconnected from their power source. Gradually the glow fades away until the light is completely extinguished. This phenomenon is similar to what happened to Adam and Eve. When they ate the forbidden fruit, they became disconnected from God and began the process of aging and eventual death. The life that God had breathed into them gradually faded over time, and their physical bodies deteriorated until they eventually passed away.

Adam and Eve lived for more than nine hundred years, but now, most people's lifespan is less than a century. God is the source of power for humanity, but we were disconnected from Him when Adam and Eve rebelled against Him. Since then, every person who has been born inherited this spiritual separation from God. Christians refer to this condition as spiritual death.

The cross made it possible for our spirits to be reconnected to God. However, our physical bodies are still waiting for redemption (Romans 8:23), which can only happen when Jesus returns for His church. At that moment, our physical being will be transformed "in the twinkling of an eye" (1 Corinthians 15:52). Even though our renewed spirit affects our physical being, physical death is inevitable, as our bodies are not yet connected to God, the source of life. Nevertheless, this does not mean that a Christian must die in sickness, as Christ purchased our healing with His broken body on the cross.

Romans 6:23 teaches us that the punishment for sin is death. This verse was mentioned earlier. Death can take many forms, such as depression, anxiety, and sickness. These were unknown to Adam and Eve before they sinned. Similarly, a Christian who operates from their spirit will not experience them either. In Christ, there is no room for depression or anxiety. The Holy Spirit has sealed us in Jesus (Ephesians 1:13) and can teach us how to operate from our position in Him if we make time each day to meditate on God's Word.

Chapter 15

Jesus Paid Humanity's Debt

The sea gave up the dead who were in it, and Death and Hades delivered up the dead who were in them. And they were judged, each one according to his works. Then Death and Hades were cast into the lake of fire. This is the second death. And anyone not found written in the Book of Life was cast into the lake of fire.

REVELATION 20:13–15

In the beginning, Adam and Eve sinned and were separated from God, which caused the first death. Every human being born after them inherited this spiritual separation from God, and as a result, humanity lost access to God. Death began to manifest itself in the form of poverty, sickness, and murder. However, Jesus Christ opened the way for us to be reconnected to God at the cross. At the cross, we were redeemed from the curse of the fall, which consists of spiritual death, poverty, and sickness.

Sickness, depression, and anxiety are all examples of the progression of spiritual death in the physical realm. Left unchecked, each will ultimately lead to physical death. Those who do not accept the redemptive work of Jesus will be judged after this life and cast into the lake of fire. This is the "second death" that is mentioned in Revelation 20:14. The cross provides us opportunity to escape from being eternally separated from God in the lake of fire, but we must choose to turn to Jesus. God will not force any person to do this.

Jesus Paid Twice What
Was Due for Our Sin

Many people believe that God's grace means He overlooks our sins, but that is untrue. God does not suddenly decide one day that sin no longer has any importance. His grace is genuine, but sin still requires judgment. As we have seen in Romans 6:23, the wage for sin is death, which was paid in full by Jesus on the cross.

God sent Jesus to Earth to pay the price for our sins. Isaiah 40:2 states that the price for sin has been paid twice, which has never happened in the physical world. Throughout history, the Jews have suffered greatly for their sins, paying double the price. However, it is prophesied in Isaiah 40 that the coming Messiah would double the price for the sins of Israel and all humanity.

Jesus paid more than what our sins deserved. Our sins deserved judgment, and God did not ignore them. Instead, He allowed His Son to be judged in our place. To understand this, imagine if you were called to court for speeding and found out that the judge was your own father. While you might expect him to show you mercy, a just judge would assess the maximum fine possible. You would undoubtedly be surprised and dismayed by the severity of the punishment you'd receive, but anything less would be unjust. But what would you do if your father stepped down from the bench, took off his robe, and then offered to either pay the fine or serve the sentence on your behalf? This is precisely what Jesus did when He paid for our sins.

Jesus Paid Our Debt with His Life

The judge who offers to pay your penalty or serve your sentence is a perfect picture of Jesus at the cross. We all deserve death for our sins, as sin has a wage that needs to be paid. God declared this from the beginning, even before Adam and Eve ate the forbidden fruit. This was further reinforced in various passages throughout the Old and New Testaments. For example, Isaiah 59:1–2:

> Behold, the LORD's hand is not shortened, that it cannot save; nor His ear heavy, that it cannot hear. But your iniquities have separated you from your God; and your sins have hidden His face from you, so that He will not hear.

Many people misquote these verses and wrongly apply them to New Testament believers. The verse lists the consequences of sin, but as Christians, we believe that Jesus paid for our sins, and we do not have to bear those consequences. Some people seem to have rebelled against God's grace because they have been misled by preachers. For example, some pastors tell their congregations that God cannot hear their prayers if they have unconfessed sins. This is not true because if God could not listen to their prayers, He would not be able to hear their confessions either.

The Fear of God

It's easy to get caught up in focusing on the blessings and grace of God, but we should also remember what we have been saved from. While many people know about God's grace, some may not fully understand it. Unfortunately, this can lead to a trend in the church where Christians lose their fear of God. *Fear*, as defined by Merriam-Webster, can mean "an unpleasant, often strong emotion caused by anticipation or awareness of danger" or "a profound reverence and awe, especially toward God."

Here are some scriptures that refer to the fear of God. Isaiah 11:1–3 is just one example:

> There shall come forth a Rod from the stem of Jesse, and a Branch shall grow out of his roots. The Spirit of the LORD

shall rest upon Him, the Spirit of wisdom and understanding, the Spirit of counsel and might, the Spirit of knowledge and of the fear of the LORD. His delight *is* in the fear of the LORD, and He shall not judge by the sight of His eyes, nor decide by the hearing of His ears.

These verses speak of Jesus and His fear of the Lord. This is a reference to His reverence and honor for God.

An example from the New Testament can be found in Acts 9:31:

Then the churches throughout all Judea, Galilee, and Samaria had peace and were edified. And walking in the fear of the Lord and in the comfort of the Holy Spirit, they were multiplied.

In this verse, we can observe that the early Christians were motivated by their fear of the Lord. This fear was not a negative thing, but rather the reason behind their continuous spiritual growth. In those times, there was a greater level of respect and reverence toward God, which is not as prevalent in churches today.

Let's consider another example from Proverbs 16:6:

In mercy and truth atonement is provided for iniquity; and by the fear of the LORD *one* departs from evil.

Recognizing the holiness of God instills a sense of fear and reverence in us, which then leads to a life of separation from evil. In my opinion, the lack of reverence for God that was seen in the early days of Christianity is one of the reasons why there is so much evil in the world today. I have heard many Christians speak about prophecies regarding God wiping away the evil in our world and turning things around. However, this will not happen until we first restore our sense of awe and reverence that is sorely missing.

Where Fear Is Missing, Sin Increases

Sin is being celebrated in many places around the world. There are parades that are solely focused on promoting sinful behavior, and unfortunately, this has become an accepted norm in our society. However, such practices are considered abominable by God, and it is the responsibility of the church to address them. As believers, we have been given authority by God, but it seems like we are not living up to our potential. Until we start to revere God and demonstrate His power and kingdom as we have been called to do, real change will not come.

Psalm 36:1 states that the wicked have "no fear of God before [their] eyes." This once again emphasizes the connection between sin and the absence of the fear of God. When we witness people living in sin, it is often because they lack the fear of God. The problem lies in the way we proclaim the gospel message, which has led people to turn away from God and His church.

The unchecked spread of sin in the world is a consequence of the lack of fear of God. I have encountered many nonbelievers who think this life is the only one they will ever have. They do not understand the concept of eternal life. Some Christians even argue that hell is a metaphor used in the Bible and does not represent a real place. However, without hell, there can be no punishment or accountability for sins committed.

Chapter 16

The Undeserved
Goodness of God

*For the wages of sin is death, but the gift of God
is eternal life in Christ Jesus our Lord.*

ROMANS 6:23

For those who do not accept the message of the cross, there is only a performance-based relationship with God waiting. This is the same kind of relationship that was available during the Old Testament times. However, this kind of relationship cannot lead to our salvation. The cost of sin was too high for us to pay, and it is astounding that many people are still trying to pay it. In the new covenant, this is even worse because Jesus has already paid the price by going to the cross.

There is a place called hell that is mentioned over sixty-three times in the Old Testament. Although our English translations uses words like *pit* or *grave*, they are all referring to hell. Each reference is translated from the Hebrew word *Sheol*, which was the resting place of dead spirits. The term *grave* almost always refers to the place where godly people went, while the words *pit* or *hell* are used to describe the destination of those who lived without God.

The Two Compartments of Sheol

There are several scriptures that mention Sheol, which is often depicted as being located at the center of the earth. It's a place of torment, but those who turn to Jesus will be spared from it. Personally, I believe that hell is divided into two parts and is located at the center of the earth. This is clearly evident in the account of Lazarus and the rich man, which can be found in Luke 16:19–31:

> "There was a certain rich man who was clothed in purple and fine linen and fared sumptuously every day. But there was a certain beggar named Lazarus, full of sores, who was laid at his gate, desiring to be fed with the crumbs which fell from the rich man's table. Moreover the dogs came and licked his sores. So it was that the beggar died, and was carried by the angels to Abraham's bosom. The rich man also died and was buried. And being in torments in Hades, he lifted up his eyes and saw Abraham afar off, and Lazarus in his bosom. Then he cried and said, 'Father Abraham, have mercy on me, and send Lazarus that he may dip the tip of his finger in water and cool my tongue; for I am tormented in this flame.' But Abraham said, 'Son, remember that in your lifetime you received your good things, and likewise Lazarus evil things; but now he is comforted and you are tormented. And besides all this, between us and you there is a great gulf fixed, so that those who want to pass from here to you cannot, nor can those from there pass to us.' Then he said, 'I beg you therefore, father, that you would send him to my father's house, for I have five brothers, that he may testify to them, lest they also come to this place of torment.' Abraham said to him, 'They have Moses and the prophets;

let them hear them.' And he said, 'No, father Abraham; but if one goes to them from the dead, they will repent.' But he said to him, 'If they do not hear Moses and the prophets, neither will they be persuaded though one rise from the dead.'"

It is a common misconception to consider death as the end of our lives. According to James 2:26, our body is lifeless without the spirit. This means that our body and spirit separate at the time of death. The spirit and soul depart from our physical body after we die. Before the crucifixion of Jesus, those who passed away were either sent to hell or Abraham's bosom. After Jesus died, He "descended into the lower parts of the earth" (Ephesians 4:9) and then led those in Abraham's bosom to heaven (Ephesians 4:8).

Jesus freed the souls in Sheol's part known as Abraham's bosom. The area was used to hold those who passed away before Christ's crucifixion. The only part of Sheol left now is where the wicked spirits go, which is known as hell. This place is believed to be a site of torment, and it will be emptied during the Great White Throne judgment mentioned in Revelation 20:11. Anyone whose name is not in the Book of Life mentioned in Revelation 20:15 will be judged and sent to this place. Hell will cease to exist at this point.

Heaven and hell are temporary holding sites. According to Revelation 21, Christians will remain in heaven until just after the Millennial Reign, after which the planet will expire, and the new heaven and earth will be established. After this, they believe that they will live on the new earth and in the new Jerusalem for eternity. "God will wipe away every tear" when they arrive (Revelation 21:4), and Satan will be cast into the lake of fire for eternity (Revelation 20:10).

Our Value Is in Christ Alone

In Romans 6:23, we see that sin has a wage requirement: death. However, this verse is not just referring to big sins like murder or adultery. According to James 2:10, even the person who commits one violation of the Law will be guilty of the whole Law. We tend to categorize and rate sins, but God does not view them that way. He judges every sin equally, regardless of how we perceive them.

I have often heard people boasting about all the good deeds they have done for God, especially at the altar during prayer. However, we must remember that God is not like Santa Claus. He does not keep a list of our good or bad deeds. Our worth and standing before Him are solely based on the blood of Jesus that was shed on the cross. Therefore, there is nothing we can do to increase or decrease our value in His eyes. It is solely based on our acceptance of Jesus that we are saved and have eternal life.

To truly appreciate the grace of God, it's important to understand the cost that was paid to make it possible. The judgment of sin required a person who was pure and untainted by sin. Therefore, God had to take on human form, and that's where Jesus comes in. Jesus was God in the flesh, and His life was worth more than all the people who have ever existed or will exist. With just one drop of His blood, Jesus paid the price for every sin committed by any man or woman who has ever lived.

Understanding the price that Jesus paid gives us a clear understanding of grace. It also enables us to see how a holy God can love us without compromising His holiness. God didn't just wake up one day and decide to accept unholy human beings into His presence randomly. He satisfied all the demands of justice to make us holy, and we can experience this through the death of His Son on the cross, paying the wage due for sin.

God does not just look at our physical body or soul. These have not yet been redeemed. Our spirit, though, is. According to Paul, it has been recreated, and we are therefore new creations birthed in Christ Jesus (2 Corinthians 5:17). Every Christian has had their spirit recreated, and they are as holy and righteous as Jesus is in their spirit. We see this in 2 Corinthians 5:21:

> For He made Him who knew no sin to be sin for us, that we might become the righteousness of God in Him.

In John 4:24, Jesus told the woman with the issue of blood that "God *is* spirit." He emphasized that God does not judge us based on our outward appearance or emotional state. Jesus became unrighteous so that we could become righteous. In the spiritual sense, we are pure and holy. According to 1 John 4:17, we are exactly like Jesus. This verse is not talking about a future event; rather, it's referring to our present state. Our spirits have been reborn and are now identical to Jesus.

Spirit to Spirit

God is a spirit. It is only through the spirit that we can access our relationship with Him. Every provision He has made comes through our spirit. Our flesh has yet to be redeemed (Romans 8:18–25). The performance-based approach commonly used to gain favor with God is based on a part of our being that is yet to be perfected. God cannot accept us in any way other than the condition of our spirit, which is based solely on Christ.

Many people who have become born-again Christians haven't learned how to approach God from their spirit. Instead, they try to approach Him based on their actions, such as regular Bible study, church attendance, or good deeds. Although these are all good things, attempting to gain a higher standing with God based on them is considered carnal, according to the Bible. The sooner we accept the fact that our fleshly efforts will never be good enough, the sooner we will be able to enter the rest God desires for all His children.

Romans 7:18 states that our flesh lacks any goodness. In this context, the term *good* refers to anything that comes from God and is strengthened by Him through faith. Whenever we receive something from God, it is first deposited in our spirit and then flows outward through our soul into the physical realm. We can never receive anything from Him that originates in the natural realm. This is an important truth that many people tend to overlook. Our approach to God should be based solely on the cross. Unfortunately, many Christians struggle in their walk with God because they fail to understand this fundamental truth.

Chapter 17

Mixture in the Church

And He said to them, "You are those who justify yourselves
before men, but God knows your hearts. For what is highly
esteemed among men is an abomination in the sight of God."

LUKE 16:15

Many Christians today are heavily influenced by the world through various mediums such as television, books, magazines, and social media. This has led to the church adopting several values and ways of the world, which is a sad situation. Jesus had warned the Pharisees that the things valued by the world are an "abomination" in the eyes of God. It's hard to imagine what He would think of the prevailing condition of the church in today's world.

I use the internet daily for work and come across various headlines. It's surprising to see what's being reported these days. Some stories are utterly false, while others are just rumors. Unfortunately, society is obsessed with such news, and even many Christians indulge in them. I often receive prayer requests from people who are depressed after spending hours reading these headlines. While I pray for them, I also advise them that they cannot be delivered from their depression until they stop reading these headlines first.

We often idolize movie stars, athletes, and television personalities, even when their actions go against our moral and religious values.

While I hold nothing against these people and pray for them, I am shocked to see so many Christians lifting them up as role models. My hope is that, one day, we will open our eyes to see the true nature of their actions and realize how they go against God's teachings.

The Rich Man and Lazarus

In the previous chapter, I mentioned the story of a wealthy man and Lazarus (Luke 16:19–31). The story portrays the rich man as someone who dressed in expensive clothes and hosted extravagant parties every day. People probably admired him, just as our society today idolizes the rich and famous. I can even envision people lining up to get onto his guest list, and those who likely stood and praised him at his funeral. However, Jesus teaches us God's perspective. In life, the rich man was exalted, but when he died, his body was thrown into the ground to decompose just like any other person. He ended up being tormented in hell and probably forgotten by those who received his lavish inheritance.

The story also tells us about a beggar who used to eat table scraps and sat at the gate of a rich man, begging for alms. When he died, angels came to meet him and carried him into Abraham's bosom, the second compartment of Sheol that we have already discussed. Although society did not value the beggar during his life, God honored him in death. This reminds us that only the things that God honors should matter to us.

When a celebrity passes away, people often talk about the significance of losing them. However, if they leave this earth without first receiving Jesus, they will be damned to hell. It doesn't matter how accomplished, wealthy, or famous they were; nothing can change this simple truth. While we may honor and esteem these people, God sees things differently. It is time for the church to start viewing things through His eyes. This can only be possible if we first turn back to His Word.

The Goats and Sheep

I believe that we should place a much higher value on our salvation. As we have seen in James 2:10, anyone who fails in even the smallest area of the Law is guilty of violating the whole thing. There is not a single person who has succeeded in meeting the requirements of the Law. Every human being since Adam and Eve has been born into this life with a one-way ticket to hell. The only way to change our destination is by receiving Jesus as our Savior.

It's incredible how short our time on Earth is when compared to eternity. I find it puzzling that people tend to focus so much on impressing others rather than impressing God. The individuals who earn the highest incomes in our society are often athletes, movie stars, and corrupt politicians and businesspeople. However, I believe that this reality would change if more people had a revelation of the concepts we have been discussing in this book.

In Luke 16:23, we are told that the rich man "lifted up his eyes" in hell. This indicates that hell is a very real place. Although some may teach otherwise, they are contradicting Scripture. According to Matthew 25:31–46, God will separate the righteous "sheep" from the unrighteous "goats" at the end of the world. The goats will be cast into hell, which was prepared for the devil and his angels, not for humanity. It was never God's intention for any person to be sent to hell, but sin made it a necessity.

No One Will Accidentally End Up in Hell

It is believed that any person who ends up in hell must overcome several obstacles set up by God to get there. These challenges may include the person's own conscience or individuals sent by God to help guide them in the right direction. No one will accidentally end up in hell, as it is believed that there are several warning signs and opportunities to change one's ways before it's too late.

I have noticed that when I teach about the possibility of those who have never heard the gospel message ending up in hell, there is often someone in the crowd who disagrees. They question whether a holy God would allow this to happen. However, we can find an answer to this in Romans 1:18–20:

> For the wrath of God is revealed from heaven against all ungodliness and unrighteousness of men, who suppress the truth in unrighteousness, because what may be known of God is manifest in them, for God has shown it to them. For since the creation of the world His invisible attributes are clearly seen, being understood by the things that are made, even His eternal power and Godhead, so that they are without excuse.

This passage indicates that God reveals Himself to everyone, regardless of their ungodly and unrighteous behavior. This implies that every individual has an inherent knowledge of God, embedded within their consciousness. Several studies have demonstrated that even remote tribes possess some level of understanding of a triune God, before any missionary could reach them. Our God is just and faithful and provides each person with an opportunity to avoid hell before departing from this world. No individual, from Adam and Eve onward, will ever be able to stand before God and claim that they were not given a chance to turn to Him.

Many atheists and agnostics state that they have no belief in the existence of God. However, this may not be entirely true. Some people may be playing a mind game with themselves, while others may have seared their conscience to the point where they cannot accept the things of God. However, it is important to note that at some point before they became an atheist or an agnostic, God may have revealed Himself to them. Having spoken to many self-proclaimed atheists or agnostics, I have found that almost all of them are not as convinced of God's non-existence as they might lead on.

Physical Characteristics of the Dead

In the previous chapter, we analyzed the story of the rich man and Lazarus, found in Luke 16:19–31. Did you notice that verse 23 mentions the rich man "lifted up his eyes and saw Abraham"? This implies that even after death, we may still have some form of perception. Let's explore verses 23–24 to gain further insights.

> "And being in torments in Hades, he lifted up his eyes and saw Abraham afar off, and Lazarus in his bosom. Then he cried and said, 'Father Abraham, have mercy on me, and send Lazarus that he may dip the tip of his finger in water and cool my tongue; for I am tormented in this flame.'"

In this account, the rich man was suffering in hell and could see Abraham in paradise. The man was extremely thirsty and begged Lazarus to bring him just a drop of water to cool his tongue. He could also feel the heat of the flames that were tormenting him, which meant that he still had physical sensations and emotions. From this story, it can be inferred that our souls are similar to our bodies. We will be able to recognize people's souls in heaven, which will have physical attributes such as eyes, ears, and fingers, just like our bodies do. Our bodies fit like a glove over our soul and spirit, and the soul fits in the body just like our hand fits in a glove.

Another noteworthy excerpt from this story is found in verse 25, which reads, "Son, remember…" Abraham was addressing the rich man from paradise, reminding him of the life he lived on Earth. I think it is significant that people in hell and heaven will have memories of this life. This makes me think the people in hell will also remember every time God spoke to them and gave them an opportunity to turn to Him. There are people today who are tormented by thoughts of the mistakes they have made in this life. Think about what it will be like for those in hell with the ability to recall the moments they rejected God. Can you imagine suffering in the fires of hell, feeling yourself being burned by unquenchable flame, with memories of God attempting to provide you a means of escape?

There are many people who pour their entire life into becoming successful in things like business, sports, or politics. They chase fame instead of God without any thought to how short this life is. We all can turn to God. Those who do will find He provided a means to escape hell at the cross. Jesus paid the wages of our sin, and now God only asks that we believe in our hearts and confess Jesus as our Lord to be born again (Romans 10:10). If you do this, you will be assured an escape from the torments of hell and an entrance into heaven.

Chapter 18

It Is Finished

*After this, Jesus, knowing that all things were now accomplished,
that the Scripture might be fulfilled, said, "I thirst!" Now
a vessel full of sour wine was sitting there; and they filled a
sponge with sour wine, put it on hyssop, and put it to His
mouth. So when Jesus had received the sour wine, He said, "It
is finished!" And bowing His head, He gave up His spirit.*

JOHN 19:28–30

Many Christians believe that Jesus completed His work when He said, "It is finished!" However, there was still more to accomplish even after His physical suffering. According to Ephesians 4:7–10, Jesus descended "into the lower parts of the earth" after His physical death and then "led captivity captive." This means that He had to endure hell, preach to those who were in Paradise, and then lead all those who accepted Him as their Savior to freedom. After His resurrection, Jesus appeared to Mary Magdaline and made an interesting statement, found in John 20:17:

> Jesus said to her, "Do not cling to Me, for I have not yet ascended to My Father; but go to My brethren and say to them, 'I am ascending to My Father and your Father, and to My God and your God.'"

This statement caught my attention because Jesus appeared to His disciples on the same day. However, when Mary Magdalene tried to touch Him, He didn't let her, as He had not yet ascended to heaven to present His blood on the heavenly mercy seat (Hebrews 9). Later on, when He appeared to His disciples, Jesus allowed them to touch Him. This indicates that at some point between His appearance to Mary Magdalene and His appearance to the disciples, He ascended to heaven.

Christ Became a Curse on the Cross

Jesus had to still descend to hell, lead the captives to freedom, and present His blood in heaven when He said, "It is finished!" and lowered His head on the cross. There are several things He could have been referring to as finished. I believe Jesus was referring to the Old Testament Law and the way it imputed sin, causing a curse to come on humanity, based on Deuteronomy 21:22–23:

> "If a man has committed a sin deserving of death, and he is put to death, and you hang him on a tree, his body shall not remain overnight on the tree, but you shall surely bury him that day, so that you do not defile the land which the LORD your God is giving you as an inheritance; for he who is hanged is accursed of God."

This verse is cited in various other passages in the Bible. God knew beforehand that Jesus would be crucified on a tree, and this verse triggered a series of events that led to God being able to pour out His wrath on Jesus while He hung on the cross. This is the only logical reason why God would declare a curse on anyone who was hanged on a tree, in my opinion.

The Law Prepared the Way for Christ

The Law was necessary for several reasons, but its main purpose was to demonstrate to humanity that our self-righteous works could never earn us an audience with God. Our efforts will always fall short because only someone capable of fulfilling all 600+ commands contained in the Law could meet its demands. Even failing in the smallest point of the Law was considered a disqualification. It was impossible for any person to meet the Law's requirements.

The Law set such a high standard that it was impossible for any man or woman to meet it. This led to despair, as it made salvation unattainable through human effort. It is surprising to see how many people still miss this point and fall back into a works-based mindset. Some ministers even preach a works-based relationship with God, showing a lack of understanding of the message of the cross.

In the past, God gave us laws to follow. If anyone failed to observe them, corresponding judgment followed, which is clearly mentioned in Deuteronomy 28. The reason for these laws was to demonstrate that we needed a sinless Savior and had to prepare the way for Christ. Jesus was sinless and was able to sacrifice Himself on the cross, which allowed God to pour out His wrath and judgment, opening the door for our redemption. He did this by putting all the judgment and wrath that was written in the Law for our sins on the cross of Christ. Paul explained to us that God was able to wipe out "the handwriting of requirements that was against us" by nailing them to the cross (Colossians 2:14).

Our Judgment Was Placed on Jesus

John wrote about Jesus prophesying His death and resurrection in chapter 12 of his Gospel. A statement made by Jesus in John 12:28–33 shows us that He understood the judgment for our sins would be poured out on Him:

> "Father, glorify Your name." Then a voice came from heaven, saying, "I have both glorified it and will glorify it again." Therefore the people who stood by and heard it said that it had thundered. Others said, "An angel has spoken to Him." Jesus answered and said, "This voice did not come because of Me, but for your sake. Now is the judgment of this world; now the ruler of this world will be cast out. And I, if I am lifted up from the earth, will draw all peoples to Myself." This He said, signifying by what death He would die.

This passage is often cited by the supporters of the church growth movement. They commonly interpret that Jesus meant to tell His disciples that He would attract people to Himself if they presented Him in the right way. This is the way most people present these verses, and I, too, followed this approach early in my ministry.

I started to notice over time that people were not being drawn to the churches as they should be if we are interpreting the verses correctly. There are pastors who stand faithfully behind their pulpits week after week in front of congregations that experience only minimal amounts of growth. The Holy Spirit drew my attention to this, which got me questioning the common interpretation. What I found totally surprised me.

I realized that I had previously separated verse 32 from the rest of the passage without considering the context. In this verse, Jesus says that if He is lifted up, He will draw all people to Himself. However, this verse must be understood in the context of the entire passage (vv. 28–33). Jesus is talking about judgment. For instance, in verse

31, He tells those present that "now is the judgment of this world." He is not referring to something God is going to do, but rather to something that God is already in the process of doing.

According to the Bible, God had decided to bring judgment upon the world. However, instead of punishing every individual alive, He sent His Son, Jesus, as a sacrificial lamb. Jesus would act as our substitute and take upon himself the judgment that was meant for us while he hung on the cross. This event is what is referred to in John 12:32–33 (KJV):

> And I, if I be lifted up from the earth, will draw all men
> unto me. This he said, signifying what death he should die.

In most modern translations of the Bible, the word *men* has been added by the translators. However, if you look at the original language, you will see that Jesus wasn't encouraging His followers to simply glorify Him before the world and hope that the masses would be drawn to Him. In the context of the whole passage, it becomes clear that Jesus was referring to the judgment that would come upon Him when He was lifted up on the cross.

Jesus Is Our Shelter from God's Wrath

Jesus acted in a manner similar to a lightning rod while hanging on the cross. A lightning rod is always placed in a position that will allow it to draw the energy from a lightning strike, protecting the structure on which it is installed. Likewise, the Lord was lifted up on the cross and absorbed all the punishment of God's wrath, providing protection for all who choose to shelter in Him.

All of God's judgment for eternity was placed on Jesus. Every sin, past, present, and future, was poured out on Jesus at the cross. He took the wrath and punishment of God for all sin into "His own body on the tree, that we, having died to sins, might live for righteousness" (1 Peter 2:24). This is what Jesus referred to when He said, "It is finished!" just before He died. God's wrath had been poured out, and His anger against our sin had been satisfied. There were no more requirements for humanity to be redeemed. It truly was finished for all time!

Chapter 19

Peace on Earth

Now there were in the same country shepherds living out in the
fields, keeping watch over their flock by night. And behold, an
angel of the Lord stood before them, and the glory of the Lord shone
around them, and they were greatly afraid. Then the angel said to
them, "Do not be afraid, for behold, I bring you good tidings of
great joy which will be to all people. For there is born to you this
day in the city of David a Savior, who is Christ the Lord. And this
will be the sign to you: You will find a Babe wrapped in swaddling
cloths, lying in a manger." And suddenly there was with the angel
a multitude of the heavenly host praising God and saying: "Glory
to God in the highest, and on earth peace, goodwill toward men!"

LUKE 2:8–14

The angels did not declare "peace" among men when they appeared to the shepherds. Jesus did not come in human form to bring peace among men. He came to open the door for there to be peace from God toward humanity. This was accomplished when He hung on the cross and had all of God's wrath and judgment poured out on Him. God paid for all sin for all time with the blood of Jesus that was poured out on the cross.

Jesus paid for all sins—past, present, and future. Even if we have not committed a sin, it has been paid for. The penalty for all sins has been satisfied, and they are forgiven even before they are committed. The writer of Hebrews tells us that Jesus entered "the Most Holy

Place once for all" and "obtained eternal redemption" for humanity (Hebrews 9:12). This means that we are eternally redeemed, and there is no need to try to earn redemption every time we sin.

You Were Perfected at the Cross

The payment that Jesus made at the cross has perfected us for all time. As human beings, we consist of three parts—spirit, soul, and body. While we wait for the redemption of our bodies (Romans 8:23), it is the implanted Word of God that must "save" our souls (James 1:21) by renewing them with the Word of God. However, our spirits have already been recreated (2 Corinthians 5:17) and sealed into Christ (Ephesians 1:13) the moment we accepted Him as our Lord and Savior. The writer of Hebrews describes the current position of the born-again spirit in Hebrews 12:22–24:

> But you have come to Mount Zion and to the city of the living God, the heavenly Jerusalem, to an innumerable company of angels, to the general assembly and church of the firstborn *who are* registered in heaven, to God the Judge of all, to the spirits of just men made perfect, to Jesus the Mediator of the new covenant, and to the blood of sprinkling that speaks better things than *that of* Abel.

Our physical bodies are not flawless, but our spirits are. When a person accepts Jesus as their Lord and Savior, their spirit is perfected for all eternity. The price for all sins has been paid through Jesus, and sin has been fully addressed.

Jesus Paid the Price for All Sin for All Time

Daniel received a prophecy delivered by Gabriel regarding Jesus' coming that is found in Daniel 9:24:

> Seventy weeks are determined for your people and for your
> holy city, to finish the transgression, *to make an end of*
> *sins*, to make reconciliation for iniquity, to bring in ever-
> lasting righteousness to seal up vision and prophecy, and
> to anoint the Most Holy. (Emphasis added)

You may be wondering why I am mentioning this prophecy now. Pay attention to the phrase *to make an end of sins*. It connects to our discussion about how God's wrath was poured out on Jesus during His crucifixion. This means that the punishment for all the sins committed by humanity for all time, including the sins that you haven't committed yet, was included in Jesus' sacrifice. He took on himself the judgment for all sins, just as we discussed in the previous chapter.

Jesus paid the price for our sins, and through our faith in Him, we are buried and resurrected with Him, as Colossians 2:11–15 explains:

> In Him you were also circumcised with the circumcision
> made without hands, by putting off the body of the sins
> of the flesh, by the circumcision of Christ, buried with
> Him in baptism, in which you also were raised with *Him*
> through faith in the working of God, who raised Him
> from the dead. And you, being dead in your trespasses
> and the uncircumcision of your flesh, He has made alive
> together with Him, having forgiven you all trespasses, hav-
> ing wiped out the handwriting of requirements that was
> against us, which was contrary to us. And He has taken it
> out of the way, having nailed it to the cross. Having dis-
> armed principalities and powers, He made a public spec-
> tacle of them, triumphing over them in it.

The phrase *handwriting of requirements* pertains to the laws in the Old Testament. Unfortunately, many Christians have been deceived by Satan into believing that certain parts of the Law still apply to the body of Christ today. This belief has become so widespread that some ministers even teach that God's love for us increases based on our ability to adhere to the Law's requirements. They are wrong!

The Law Could Not Save Humanity

The Law provided people with the knowledge of sin, which eventually led to their realization of their need for Jesus. However, the Law alone could never justify anyone. Trying to approach God solely through the Law may lead you to doubt His willingness to accept you. It's important to understand that God sees us through the completed work of Christ. To attain freedom, we must renew our minds and see ourselves as He does—through our identity in Christ Jesus.

Religious tradition emphasizes the importance of self-effort to guide our relationship with God. However, Jesus told His disciples that our traditions make "the word of God of no effect" (Mark 7:13), which suggests that focusing solely on ourselves can hinder our connection with God. Attempting to approach God based solely on our religious efforts can lead us to turn our backs on the cross and pursue the Law instead. This can lead to death and condemnation, as the Law alone cannot bring salvation. It is important to recognize when this is happening and to focus on God rather than just our own efforts.

Before Jesus' coming, people used to compare themselves to others based on what they had done for God. This often led to a sense of superiority or inferiority based on their religious works. For instance, if you saw a homeless beggar on the street, you might feel more righteous than them because they are not doing what you are doing to serve God. However, this kind of comparison is not fair, as it ignores the fact that everyone has different circumstances and abilities. It was for this reason that the Law existed before Jesus, to help people understand their duties toward God and others, but it was not a perfect system.

God gave the Law to remove self-righteousness from us by design-ing it in a way that revealed our inability to approach Him without help. Jesus was sent to provide that assistance. The Law was intended to convict humanity and make us feel guilty, with the goal of com-pelling us to rely on His mercy. God wanted us to stop trusting in ourselves and acknowledge our helplessness, which would lead us to throw ourselves entirely on His mercy. The cross opened the door for us to do just that.

Chapter 20

The Law and the Cross

But we know that the law is good if one uses it lawfully, knowing this: that the law is not made for a righteous person, but for the lawless and insubordinate, for the ungodly and for sinners, for the unholy and profane, for murderers of fathers and murderers of mothers, for manslayers, for fornicators, for sodomites, for kidnappers, for liars, for perjurers, and if there is any other thing that is contrary to sound doctrine, according to the glorious gospel of the blessed God which was committed to my trust.

1 TIMOTHY 1:8–11

There are individuals who advocate for living a holy life and adhering to church rules, but they fail to comprehend the true meaning of the cross. However, they unknowingly end up condemning themselves by holding this stance. In my experience, people who preach strict adherence to the Law will always change their tune if challenged to show how they are able to do it. It was impossible for anyone to follow the Law before the cross, and it remains impossible even today.

I once had a professor in Bible college who believed that we need to earn God's favor through our self-righteous works. He advocated for specific spiritual disciplines such as faithfully attending church, partaking of communion, and daily reading of Scripture to maintain our position before God. One day, this professor even shared a story of sitting on the floor of his two boys' room while they slept and pleading with God that either one might be found worthy of one day earning His favor so they might be saved. This mindset is what Christ died on the cross to set us free from.

The Law Is Not for the Christian

There are some people who claim that you need to do something for God before He will be pleased with you. They often use phrases like "God can't use you unles…", "God won't bless you unless…", or "God's anointing won't work for you unless…." However, these people lack an understanding of the message of the cross and the nature of God's relationship with humanity. They do not realize that the Law was never given with the expectation that anyone could keep it completely, except for Jesus. Jesus was the only person who has ever kept the Law without failing in even one point.

In 1 Timothy 1:9, Paul tells us that the Law is not meant for a righteous person. This means that once we become born again and accept Jesus as our Lord, we are created in true righteousness and holiness, as mentioned in Ephesians 4:24. As Christians, we are made righteous in Christ Jesus and are set free from the demands of the Law. However, Satan will always try to shift our focus from Christ to self-effort, which is essentially a return to the Law.

It is crucial to understand that the Law was not given to those who have accepted Jesus. The Law was given "for *the* lawless and insubordinate, for *the* ungodly and sinners, for *the* unholy and profane, for murderers of fathers and murderers of mothers, for manslayers, for fornicators, for sodomites, for kidnappers, for liars, for perjurers" (1 Timothy 1:9–10). God's purpose in giving the Law to Moses was to bring the ungodly to their knees in repentance. He desires every person to turn away from their ungodliness and turn toward Jesus.

Double Jeopardy

Christ has redeemed us from the curse of the law, having become a curse for us (for it is written, "Cursed is everyone who hangs on a tree"), that the blessing of Abraham might come upon the Gentiles in Christ Jesus, that we might receive the promise of the Spirit through faith. (Galatians 3:13–14)

The Law's curse was nailed to the cross (Colossians 2:14). Jesus absorbed its demands and punishments, suffering for us to experience His righteousness.

In natural legal systems, a double jeopardy principle states that an individual cannot be prosecuted twice for the same crime. This principle is also applicable to the Christian belief system. According to it, all humans were put on trial, with Jesus being our substitute. We were declared guilty, and Jesus took upon himself the punishment that we deserved. However, some Christians express anxiety about God's getting angry with them, but they fail to grasp the idea of double jeopardy. The crucifixion of Jesus satisfied all the requirements of heaven's justice system, and no human being can be put on trial again for the sin of our transgressions.

In natural court systems, it is impossible to be tried for the same offense more than once. Similarly, in heaven's court, it is equally impossible. Jesus stood for us and was found guilty for our past, present, and future sins. He paid the penalty with His life on the cross and then suffered the torment of hell on our behalf. Therefore, we cannot be punished for something that Jesus has already been punished for. As He was separated from the Father, there is no legal justification for us to be separated from Him.

Paul states in Romans 8:1 that there is no condemnation for those who are in Christ Jesus. This means that Jesus took upon Himself the condemnation that we deserved. When we suffer from condemnation, we are bearing something that Jesus has already carried for us. The Lord cried out, "My God, My God, why have You forsaken Me?" because He became sin in our place (Matthew 27:46; 2 Corinthians 5:21). Jesus didn't just take a small amount of sin to make a symbolic payment; rather, He took all the sins that will ever be committed by any human who will ever live for all time into His body when it was nailed to the cross. The Law, for the purpose of righteousness, is now ended, as its requirements were satisfied by Jesus. As Christians, we should not be living under a works mentality ever again.

Sin Is Not the Main Issue

Over the years, I have spoken with many people who routinely pray and seek something from God. They know it is God's will for them to receive it. However, most of them question whether they are worthy of receiving it. In reality, they are right. We don't deserve anything from God based on our own merit. This is the reason why Jesus was punished and bore the penalty we owed. All our sins were placed on Him and nailed to the cross.

A great exchange took place when our sins were placed on Jesus. At that moment, all of His righteousness was credited to our accounts. This exchange occurred almost two thousand years before we were born. Jesus did not deserve to bear our sins, and we did not deserve to receive His righteousness. He was holy, and it was not right for Him to take on our sins, but He willingly did so. In the same way, we do not deserve to receive His righteousness, but we have it. Just as surely as He took our sins, we have now been given His righteousness.

If you have accepted Jesus as the Lord of your life, then your spirit is just as righteous, holy, and pure as Jesus'. I believe that it is not right for people to carry a sense of guilt and unworthiness into their relationship with God. This often manifests in phrases like, "I am so unworthy of Your love," during prayers. I have heard such statements being made by people during church services, and it always makes me uncomfortable. These statements do not honor Jesus or the sacrifice He made on the cross.

According to Daniel 9:24, sin was put to an end at the cross. This means that our individual sins are no longer the main issue. However, I have observed that many Christians tend to focus more on their sins rather than Jesus' righteousness, which has been credited to their accounts. While sin is still a relevant issue today, it is important to recognize that it opens a door for the devil to work in our lives. Therefore, leading holy lives is beneficial. However, the truth that many fail to understand is that we can live a holier life if we shift our focus from sin to what Jesus did for us on the cross. This change of focus will cause a deep love for God to grow within us, leading us to live holier lives without even trying.

The End of the Law for the Righteous

In Romans 10:4, Paul states that "Christ *is* the end of the law for righteousness to everyone who believes." This means that, as Christians, we are no longer bound by the Law. Jesus fulfilled all its requirements, and now we live in His righteousness. This is why Paul urged his readers to stand fast therefore in the liberty by which Christ has made us free, and do not be entangled again with a yoke of bondage (Galatians 5:1). Here, the "yoke" refers to the Old Testament Law.

I understand your concern about how many Christians have fallen into a performance-based mentality. It is contrary to what Paul taught his followers. While it is unacceptable to see anyone living in sin, it is not appropriate to tell them that God is angry with them for their actions. Unfortunately, many ministers tend to do so. Instead, Christians should not push each other into a works-based relationship with God by making statements like "God is angry with you for your sin," or "God will punish you by removing His anointing." Statements like this are lies from the pit of hell.

It is important to understand that God does not hold anger toward us for our mistakes and sins. In fact, He loves us so much that He sent His Son, Jesus, to die on the cross and take the punishment for our sins. Some people might say that God punished a minister who fell into sin and lost their ministry, but this is not accurate. Jesus already took the punishment for our sins, so losing the ministry would be a consequence of the minister's actions, not a punishment from God. However, it is worth noting that sin can open the door for Satan to enter our lives and cause trouble, so it is important to stay vigilant and avoid sin whenever possible. Nonetheless, in order to walk in the liberty provided in Christ Jesus, it is essential to understand that God does not cause our problems and troubles.

Chapter 21

Christ's Righteousness Alone

*Brethren, my heart's desire and prayer to God for Israel
is, that they might be saved. For I bear them record that they
have a zeal of God, but not according to knowledge.*

ROMANS 10:1–2 (KJV)

There are many ministers who have good intentions and a passion for serving God but lack the knowledge of the truth. Due to the lack of revelation knowledge, they unknowingly lead their congregations back to legalism. I was one of those people before I developed a personal relationship with the Holy Spirit. Like many other Christians, my perception of God was distorted because of the church my family attended when I was younger. The church presented a harsh image of God who was always quick to judge and condemn, even for the smallest of mistakes.

There is a fundamental difference between trusting in Christ's righteousness and trusting in our own goodness. People who strive to connect with God by relying on their own good deeds are essentially putting their faith in themselves. This approach is bound to fail. Any attempt to approach God by relying on our own merits is a rejection of the cross and a dangerous path to take. We have already discussed the perils of this approach in previous chapters.

Jesus Paid the Entire Price to Redeem Us

As mentioned earlier, Jesus did not sacrifice Himself on the cross to partially pay the debt for our sins. The righteousness that we stand in is not a blend of our good works and His righteousness. God made Him to be our sin so that we could become righteous through Him (2 Corinthians 5:21). It's as simple as that. You cannot do anything to become more or less righteous in the eyes of God. You are righteous because Jesus became your sin on the cross.

Jesus paid the entire debt that was due for our sins. We have two options when it comes to our relationship with Him: we can either base it on this fact or on our own goodness. There is no middle ground. Those who base their relationship with Him on His sacrifice will find themselves standing in the freedom and liberty that His death on the cross provides. However, those who continue to try and earn God's love through their own self-righteous works will miss out on this freedom. They will continue to feel condemned and held in bondage in their Christian journey. But this does not have to be their final state. If you have fallen into the trap of self-righteousness, all you need to do is humbly repent. The Holy Spirit is waiting to help you enter into the freedom and liberty that Jesus died to enable us to experience.

Jesus Is the Completion of the Law

Many Christians tend to measure their righteousness based on what they have accomplished for God rather than on what He did for them at the cross. It is quite common to hear remarks like, "I don't think I'm good enough for God to bless me," or "I'm not worthy of God's forgiveness." These statements indicate that the person is relying on their own righteousness instead of Christ's. They are following a performance-based approach to God, outside of grace. Most of them are unaware of their position.

As discussed in the previous chapters, Jesus has put an end to religion that is based on performance. He has completed the work and paid the price for our sins. The Law has no power over Christians anymore, as Jesus has fulfilled the purpose of righteousness. God's anger toward our sins has been satisfied, and now there is no division between humans and God. Jesus took our place, faced the judgment that was due to us, and opened the door for us to enter God's presence freely.

I believe that the most significant revelation you can have is that God is not angry with you. The conflict between humanity and God has been resolved. Jesus established a truce that can never be broken. Only those who refuse to accept Jesus today will have any reason to worry about the Law. They are exposed to God's anger only because of their deliberate rejection of everything that Jesus accomplished for them on the cross.

Gravity is a force that is always present and keeps us on the ground. However, an airplane is able to fly because it uses aerodynamics to counteract the force of gravity. Nevertheless, gravity still exists and can be dangerous if we disregard it. Similarly, Christ has set us free from the curse of the Law, but the Law still exists and applies to those who do not follow Christ.

Freedom from Condemnation

In Romans 8:1, it says that "*there is* therefore now no condemnation to those who are in Christ Jesus, who do not walk according to the flesh." This means that those who choose to follow the teachings of Jesus will be free from guilt and punishment. However, this is not the case for people who allow themselves to be controlled by the physical realm; they will always feel guilty and condemned, even though Jesus died to set them free from these negative feelings.

John tells us that "God did not send His Son into the world to condemn the world, but that the world through Him might be saved" (John

3:17). It does not please God to see us suffer under the condemnation Jesus died to free us from. Jesus did not willingly take our sin and then allow Himself to be nailed to the cross to see us live in bondage under the oppression of Satan. He died for us to be free, and John even tells us that any person who "believes in the Son has everlasting life" (John 3:36). He goes on to tell us that the person who "does not believe in the Son shall not see life, but the wrath of God abides on him" (John 3:36).

The Law represents God's punishment, and it still applies to those who refuse to accept grace. However, for those who have accepted Christ and everything He accomplished on the cross, it is considered complete. All our sins were transferred to Jesus, and now our connection with God is not based on our actions, but on what Jesus has done. There is a significant difference between the Law and grace, but unfortunately, the majority of Christians seem to have lost the understanding of the cross. This is why religion continues to accuse people of sinning even after they have accepted Jesus.

Final Words

In Galatians 3:19, Paul poses the question, "What purpose then *does* the law *serve?*" He then proceeds to provide the answer in the same verse, stating that the Law was added due to transgressions, until the seed (referring to Jesus) would come to whom the promise was made. The Law served to drive humanity to the realization of our need for Jesus.

As believers in Jesus, we are no longer bound by the Law. We need not constantly evaluate ourselves to determine our worth to God. Instead, our standing with Him is based on our position in Christ Jesus, which was made possible through His sacrifice on the cross. By living according to the truths presented in this book, we can experience true freedom. Christ took upon Himself the curse of our sins, and through His sacrifice, He satisfied the requirements of heaven's justice system, allowing us to walk free.

Closing Prayer

(Based on Ephesians 1:16-21)

We do not cease to give thanks for you, making mention of you in our prayers that the God of our Lord Jesus Christ, the Father of glory, may give unto each person who reads this book the spirit of wisdom and revelation in the knowledge of Him, the eyes of the understanding being enlightened to the message of the cross. We pray that you will know what is the hope of His calling, what are the riches of the glory of His inheritance in the saints, and what is the exceeding greatness of His power toward all who believe, according to the working of His mighty power, which He worked in Christ when He raised Him from the dead and seated Him at His right hand in the heavenly places, far above all principality and power and might and dominion, and every name that is named, not only in this age, but also in that which is to come.

www.ingramcontent.com/pod-product-compliance
Lightning Source LLC
Chambersburg PA
CBHW071349090426
42738CB00012B/3069